DEVELOPMENT WITH TRADE

DEVELOPMENT WITH TRADE

LDCs and the International Economy

Edited by
Anne O. Krueger

A Sequoia Seminar

ICS Press

Institute for Contemporary Studies
San Francisco, California

Development with Trade
Copyright © 1988 by Sequoia Institute

Inquiries, book orders, and catalogue requests should be addressed to ICS Press, 243 Kearny Street, San Francisco, California, 94108. (415) 981-5353.

This book is derived from the proceedings of one of the seminars in a series conducted by Sequoia Institute. Both the seminar series and this publication were funded by the United States Agency for International Development.

PDC-0092-A-00-6050-00

U.S.A.I.D.

Library of Congress Cataloging-in-Publication Data

Development with trade.

Bibliography: p.
1. Developing countries—Commerce. 2. International trade.
3. Developing countries—Economic policy. 4. Economic development. I. Kreuger, Anne O. II. Sequoia Institute.
HF4055.D49 1988 382′.09172′4 88-28460
ISBN 1-55815-042-0
ISBN 1-55815-041-2 (pbk.)

Contents

Preface

Development for emerging nations, expansion of the international economy, and the inclusion of individuals now being left out of the process of economic growth will be enhanced by a competitive market environment. The authors of this volume understand the necessity of fostering such an environment and focus on the importance of international trade to less developed countries. Furthermore, it addresses at length the possibilities for increasing world trade opportunities during the current Uruguay Round negotiations.

This publication is the third in a series from seminars conducted by Sequoia Institute. Addressing the topic *Including the Excluded: Extending the Benefits of Development*, the seminars facilitate the exchange of research, information, and ideas on issues critical to Third World development. The series examines the successes and failures of development strategies, encouraging the reexamination of established principles and, where necessary, the formulation of new ones. Additional volumes, also to be published by ICS Press, will focus on trade policies, capital markets, community, taxing, and other issues.

Robert B. Hawkins, Jr.
President & CEO
Institute for Contemporary Studies

San Francisco
October 1988

Foreword

This is the third publication resulting from a series of seminars introduced by Sequoia Institute in 1987. Expected to conclude in 1991, the series has two primary objectives:

a) to shed new light on critical issues of Third World development and its assistance, and

b) to serve as a catalyst for a new generation of thinkers and ideas that will accelerate the inclusion of *all* people in the process of individual and societal development.

The theme of the series, *INCLUDING THE EXCLUDED: Extending the Benefits of Development*, was applied in the first two seminars to the domestic circumstances of developing countries. The theme is extended in this third seminar volume to the international arena, specifically addressing the importance of expanded international trade for the development of countries.

A reading of the first three volumes in the series raises the possibility of a reciprocal, mutually reinforcing, relationship between exclusionary (e.g., protectionist) international trade policies and the domestic institutions and policies of trading countries. This suggests, in turn, that the potential for including the excluded *within* any country may be critically affected by the magnitude of exclusions *among* countries.

Sponsorship of this series by the Agency for International Development (A.I.D.) is an outgrowth of the Agency's policy endeavors during the past several years. Support for these seminars continues a commitment by the Agency to encourage the reexamination of established precepts and practices pursuant to the formulation of more effective development policies and practices. In accordance with this objective, the series strives to enlarge the supply of talent and ideas which are ordinarily applied to development issues. One component of this effort, of course, is the publication and dissemination of each seminar's proceedings for a far more inclusive audience. Another is to bring together several promising scholars who are relatively new to the international development field, by virtue of their youth or the concentration of their previous scholarship on other subject matter, for interacting with established development scholars and practitioners.

In addition to the Administrator of the Agency, Alan Woods, and Assistant Administrator, Richard E. Bissell, the support and cooperation of numerous A.I.D. personnel has been instrumental to the success of the seminar series. Within the Bureau for Program and Policy Coordination, the A.I.D. technical office most responsible for this endeavor, three project officers—Edwin L. Hullander, Warren Weinstein and Neal S. Zank—have provided encouragement and valuable technical assistance to the series since its inception. The success of this particular seminar also benefited substantially from the contributions of A.I.D.'s Office of Economic Affairs, most notably, Mike Unger and Ernest H. Preeg, the Agency's chief economist at that time.

It is the good fortune of the seminar series that Anne O. Krueger afforded the time in her busy schedule to direct this particular seminar—establishing the agenda, engaging the authors of the respective papers, moderating the seminar proceedings, and, finally, both editing and contributing to the product in these pages.

Dr. Krueger joins me in expressing appreciation to Rebecca McGovern and Julie Ellis of ICS Press and especially to Roger Magyar, our editorial assistant, for their efforts in putting the seminar materials into finished form.

Though none of the opinions expressed in this book are necessarily shared by the Agency for International Development or Sequoia Institute, it is hoped that they will stimulate the formulation of better ideas than would have otherwise occurred, and that a developing world will be the beneficiary.

Jerry Jenkins
Series Editor

Washington, DC
October, 1988

1 *Anne O. Krueger*

Introduction

The world economy is not likely to undergo another success resembling that of the period between World War II and 1973. The rate of real economic growth of world GNP far exceeded that of any quarter century in the history of mankind. Moreover, that growth was both caused by and resulted in rapid liberalization of the international trading system and an accompanying move to financial integration.

Economic historians would no doubt credit a number of factors with that phenomenal growth. However, it is unquestionable that a major contributor was the momentum provided by the international economic system and institutions established at the end of World War II. Certainly, trade liberalization accelerated the economic growth that would in any event have occurred, and economic growth created an environment that made trade liberalization possible. The presence of the General Agreement on Tariffs and Trade (GATT), the International Monetary Fund, and the World Bank facilitated the process in very important ways: had the Bretton Woods Institutions not been established, they would have had to be invented.

The buoyancy of the postwar years was somewhat diminished in the 1970s and early 1980s. Simultaneously, the momentum toward further liberalization of trade was greatly reduced, if not entirely stalled. Table 1 gives data on world trade for selected years from 1950 to 1986. It shows that if one deflates the dollar value of world trade by export unit value data, and uses that estimate as an approximate "real value" of exports, world exports doubled between 1950 and 1960 and again between 1960 and 1970. Even between 1970 and 1980, there was an increase of 80 percent; between 1980 and 1986, however, world trade hardly grew at all. By the mid-1980s, it became apparent that the world economy was probably at a crossroads: either the momentum toward further integration of the world economy would be resumed, or there would be a significant danger that the protectionist pressures that had emerged in the early 1980s would intensify and serve as a strong brake on the future growth of the international economy. While current technological advances provide great rewards to new entrants to international markets and thus increase incentives for opening of trade, the growth rate of the international economy remains a key to the prospects of all developing countries. And that growth rate, while favorably affected by technical changes, will also be greatly influenced by the extent to which protectionist pressures are reversed.

Because of the importance of the international trade and financial system to the developed countries, a great deal of attention has been paid to the need for measures to prevent disintegration of the international economy, and analysis of the pressures for protection and policies in the developed countries that might diminish these pressures.

However, between 1960 and 1985, one of the major lessons was the importance of an open and growing international trading system to the growth prospects of the developing countries. These countries had by and large been passive beneficiaries of the great liberalization and expansion of international trade between 1950 and 1973. Although they themselves had not been active participants in multilateral trade liberalization, they had de facto begun

Table 1
Growth of World Exports and Developing Countries' Exports, 1950 to 1986

	1950	1960	1970	1980	1986
World exports (bil. $)	59.9	120.6	290.4	1,896.7	1,989.4
Export unit value (1980 = 100)	23.9[a]	23.6	27.1	100.0	99.2[a]
"Real" exports[b]	250.6	511.0	1,071.6	1,896.7	2,005.4
Non-oil exporting developing countries' exports (bil. $)	19.5	29.3	52.2	335.4	383.4
Oil exporting developing countries' exports (bil. $)	4.2	7.5	16.8	301.8	n.a.

Source: International Monetary Fund, *International Financial Statistics*, 1987 Yearbook.
[a]Unit values for industrial countries only.
[b]"Real" exports are dollar exports divided by export unit values.

to liberalize their own economies over that era, starting, however, from highly restrictive trade regimes.

As discussion of mechanisms for resuming the growth of the international economy proceeded in the mid-1980s, it was clear that the developing countries not only had a major stake in the outcome, but that their position in the international economy had changed greatly. Their increased importance implied that it was, and is, highly desirable that means be found for their more active participation in the processes which affect the future of the system. Mexico's accession to the GATT and their apparent reversal of trade policies may be symptomatic of a growing shift in developing countries' policies and attitudes.

The Sequoia Institute therefore decided to hold a seminar to address the international institutions, trade, and growth of the developing countries. The hope was that by focusing on the key issues surrounding the international trading system from the viewpoint of the developing countries, there would be increased awareness of the many crucial ways in which the developing countries are not only affected by, but also affect, the international economy. Further, attention to the changed role and significance of the developing countries might elicit suggestions of measures that could be used to effect more meaningful participation by the developing countries in the international economic system.

This volume contains the proceedings of that seminar. The remainder of this introduction is devoted to providing the reader with background which may facilitate understanding of the subsequent chapters. Four topics are covered: 1) the GATT and its evolution, 2) the relationship between the less developed countries (LDCs) and the GATT, 3) the importance of an open international trading system to the developing countries, and 4) the status of the trade negotiations currently under way and the position of the developing countries in them.

GATT and its Evolution[1]

Once it became clear that World War II was being won by the Allies, consideration began of ways in which the postwar world might be structured in order to facilitate political and economic benefit for all concerned. For a variety of reasons, the English and Americans were the chief architects of the postwar system. Economists from both countries actively engaged in discussions of the ways in which the international economic system might be arranged to avoid some of the problems of earlier years—especially those of the 1930s.

The outcome of these deliberations was the Bretton Woods conference, at which representatives of most Allied nations agreed to establish three multilateral, international economic institutions. These institutions, it was envisaged, would provide an institutional framework within which economic relations between countries could evolve in a manner conducive to economic growth and efficiency. The Bretton Woods participants developed charters laying out the principles of international economic relations and the procedures by which the institutions would provide a framework for the continuing realization of these principles. Countries would sign treaties joining the institutions, thereby accepting their principles and agreeing to the procedures.

The three institutions envisioned by the participants at the Bretton Woods conference were the International Monetary Fund (IMF), the International Bank for Reconstruction and Development (IBRD), and the International Trade Organization (ITO). It was anticipated that the IMF would in effect oversee international financial relations, encouraging full currency convertibility and overseeing arrangements governing exchange rates (which were, until 1973, supposed to be fixed and changed only after negotiation with the Fund's staff to insure that countries did not adopt exchange rate policies inimical to their major trading partners). The IBRD (which subsequently evolved into the World Bank) was expected to serve as a financial intermediary, assuring an efficient allocation of capital worldwide by borrowing in markets of capital-rich countries to lend in capital-poor ones, where rates of return were expected to be higher. As its name implies, the IBRD was initially expected to devote its primary attention to the financing of postwar reconstruction, although support of development activities was also within its mandate. As it in fact evolved, it started almost entirely as an institution financing postwar reconstruction, and became almost exclusively a development institution as reconstruction was successfully accomplished.

The third institution was supposed to be the International Trade Organization. It was designed to govern international trading relations in much the same manner as the IMF was to oversee international financial relations. However, the treaty for the ITO was not passed by the U.S. Senate; instead, a General Agreement on Tariffs and Trade was negotiated and ratified. The GATT has since been the international organization with responsibility for trading relations among its signatories.[2]

As will be seen later in this volume, one of the current major questions of international economic policy concerns the relationships between the IMF, the IBRD, and the GATT. For present purposes, however, the reader should be acquainted with certain salient characteristics of the GATT.

The GATT, as founded and as it still exists, gives expression to the principles of an international trading system that were espoused by the United States and the Allies at the end of the World War II. These principles were advocated by the Americans and the English not only because it was felt that they were in their countries' self-interest, but also because it was deemed that they were in the larger global interest, as the two countries sought to create a viable international economic order. The main philosophical underpinning of the system was that the international trading system should be *nondiscriminatory*, and, to the maximum extent possible, free of restrictions to international trade. Signatories (the "contracting parties," i.e., those countries acceeding to GATT) also agreed to eschew quantitative restrictions (except in special circumstances). There were also provisions which enabled the GATT to serve as a forum for multilateral negotiations of liberalization of trade.

At the outset, GATT procedures and principles applied primarily to manufactured goods; trade in agricultural commodities was neglected, in part because the United States opposed its inclusion and had agricultural trade "grandfathered" out of the GATT, and in part because so many exceptions and exclusions were written into GATT rules, making GATT largely ineffective in agricultural trade. Trade in services was largely ignored, primarily because service trade was a very small fraction of goods trade in the early postwar years. When the GATT articles were drafted, focus on trade in manufactures was probably appropriate, since barriers to trade in manufactured commodities were undoubtedly much greater in their impact than were barriers to trade in agriculture or services.

The signatories to the GATT subscribed to a most-favored-nation (MFN) clause, under which they undertook to treat each individual trading partner in the same manner as a most favored nation, i.e., they would not treat goods being imported from one country any differently from the way they would treat goods imported from another (they did, however, agree that groups of countries forming customs unions or free-trade areas might treat other members of the union differently from those outside it).

It was also envisaged that signatories to GATT would rely only on tariffs as an instrument of protection: quantitative restrictions were to be eschewed as an instrument of commercial policy unless a country had acute, short-run, balance-of-payments difficulties. Even then, countries were expected to provide compensation to other countries which were adversely affected by the use of quantitative restrictions, and it was anticipated that countries would be subject to judicial proceedings within GATT were they to abuse the balance-of-payments clause.[3]

Under GATT, procedures were established whereby a country believing itself unfairly dealt with by another country might seek redress. This might happen if it were not given MFN treatment, if a country having "bound" its tariff under GATT then raised it because of domestic injury, or if another GATT member took measures against the GATT charter which it believed negatively affected it. There were also, however, a number of provisions pertaining to the situation of developing countries which permitted them fairly free exemption from GATT provisions.

In addition, the GATT charter provided a mechanism through which countries could mutually negotiate reciprocal tariff reductions, and then "bind"[4] those negotiated tariffs. Through this process, it was anticipated, tariff reductions could take place over time and the world could come closer and closer to free trade.[5]

Over the postwar years, GATT negotiations for tariff reductions were eminently successful. Starting with the Dillon Round of tariff negotiations in the late 1950s, and following with the Kennedy and Tokyo Rounds in the 1960s and 1970s, tariff rates among the major industrial countries were negotiated and bound at very low levels. Indeed, as early as 1970, it could be convincingly argued that nontariff barriers to trade in manufactures were a more substantial barrier to trade than were tariffs because of earlier successes in reducing tariffs.[6] Further tariff reductions were negotiated in the Tokyo Round, but major attention was focused on finding ways of addressing some important nontariff barriers to trade. Although the Tokyo Round met with some success in negotiating "codes of conduct," which members might sign and adhere to,[7] it is clear that resumption of momentum toward an open multilateral international trading system will depend on addressing significant non-tariff barriers to trade, which are now the key trade barriers among developed countries. They are important in some manufacturing industries, such as textiles and clothing, but they are also important in agriculture and services. These issues are presently being considered in the Uruguay Round of trade negotiations, which began in the fall of 1986.

Overall, the GATT was eminently successful in providing mechanisms for reductions of trade barriers against manufactured goods among the major industrial countries. And, as mentioned at the outset, the simultaneous impetus to economic growth and to trade liberalization was a vital ingredient in the "golden era" of economic growth prior to 1973.

Relations Between the GATT and LDCs

For a variety of reasons the developing countries remained on the sidelines within GATT. Even most of those that did become members in the earlier years used the GATT provisions discussed in this section to conduct trade policies widely at variance with the principles of GATT.[8]

Several factors contributed to minimizing the role of developing countries within GATT. First, their own trade policies were based on a philosophy substantially at variance with the open, multilateral principles of the GATT. Second, most developing countries' exports of manufactured commodities were relatively small, and the principal negotiations took place between major trading partners. Third, and related to the second point, the developing countries benefitted from the tariff reductions negotiated among the larger, developed countries and were thus "free riders" to the GATT benefits. Fourth and finally, developing countries began advocating "special and differential treatment" for themselves within the GATT which was manifestly inconsistent with their full participation; even within the charter they are exempt from the "reciprocity" provisions of negotiated tariff reductions which is obligatory for other participants in a GATT round of tariff negotiations.

The developing countries' insistence on "special and differential" treatment (S&D) was based on the notion that developing countries' economies were somehow "different." This difference, it was argued, made acquiescence to GATT principles incompatible with their own economic aspirations. In a sense, the argument was that developing countries' economies were weak and thus deserving of some special treatment.

Two sections of the GATT articles were used as a basis for S&D. On one hand, the GATT articles recognized the "infant-industry" case for temporary protection of a fledgling industry: Article XVIII recognized that developing countries with infant industries might protect those industries during their initial period. The infant-industry case, long since recognized by economists, essentially asserts that *if* there are likely to be significant cost reductions over time so that a newly established industry will eventually become internationally competitive, and *if* those reductions will accrue in part to others within the economy, *then* it may improve a country's economic welfare if there is a period of temporary assistance as the industry's costs fall.[9] Most governments in developing countries regarded almost all manufacturing industries as infants and therefore regarded their economies as exempt from the other GATT articles.

However, the GATT articles also provided a basis for imposition of quantitative restrictions: Article XII provides that a country may impose quantitative restrictions in the event that its "balance-of-payments situation" is so serious that it must do so. Virtually all developing countries have cited Article XII as a basis for the imposition of quantitative restrictions. This has had two important consequences: 1) it has been harmful to their own economic growth; and 2) it has served as a strong disincentive for developed countries to negotiate mutual tariff reductions with developing countries because of their concern that the developing country could escape the "binding" of the tariff by appealing to Article XII exemptions.

Over the years, developing countries chose to use their bargaining power to seek further (and apparently more favorable) special and differential treatment. For example, they sought, and attained, the Generalized System of Preferences (GSP), under which imports from developing countries of specified manufactured goods enter developed country markets either duty free or with duties assessed at a fraction of the rate applicable to imports of the comparable product from developed countries.[10] Most analysts have concluded that the limitations surrounding imports under GSP are so restrictive that GSP in practice has been worth relatively little to developing countries.[11] However, developing countries' attitudes toward negotiating MFN tariff reductions have been seriously influenced by their concern that lowered tariff rates would reduce the value of GSP to them.

An important emerging issue for the international economy is whether developing countries will continue to focus on S&D, or whether they will recognize their broader interest in resumption of the trend toward multilateral trade liberalization for the entire world economy.

Thus, many developing countries have joined the GATT but have remained de facto exempt from the GATT system. An important question is whether this state of affairs is in the self-interest of the developing countries themselves, and whether the maintenance of S&D status is consistent with the healthy expansion of the international economy which is indisputably in developing countries' interest.

The Importance of an Open International Trading System for LDCs

As the developing countries turned their attention to achieving rapid economic growth after World War II, there was a surprising degree of uniformity of views and economic policy among them regarding international trading relations. In part because of the legacy of colonialism, in part because of memories of the Great Depression, and in part because of other factors, almost all developing countries in the early 1950s rejected the notion that they might grow through reliance on comparative advantage and the international market; instead they opted for policies of "import substitution."

The underlying rationale had both a negative and a positive aspect. On the negative side, there was a widespread belief that developing countries would forever have a comparative advantage in primary commodities, the demand for which, it was thought, would grow slowly. It was therefore feared that if a developing country relied on the international market and increased consumption of importables no more rapidly than export earnings grew, the country would be forced to grow slowly—either because the volume of exports would grow relatively slowly, or because a more rapid volume growth would bring with it declining export prices and hence a much less rapid growth of export earnings than of volume.

On the positive side, it was recognized that rising per capita incomes would come about with increased productivity; increased productivity would then imply that fewer workers were needed on the land, and that the labor force would gradually become less and less concentrated in agricultural production. It was correctly concluded that a more rapid rate of growth of employment in industry than in agriculture would be a hallmark of successful industrialization; it was incorrectly concluded, however, that such industrial growth could only occur under import substitution policies. While the infant-industry rationale for encouragement was frequently cited, import substitution policies as practiced almost always gave permanent protection to domestic industries and were indiscriminately applied.[12]

Almost all developing countries adopted policies which, in effect, greatly reduced the ties between their domestic markets and the international economy. Domestic industry was then encouraged by high walls of protection against import-competing products.[13] Sometimes this took the form of quantitative restrictions on import levels once domestic productive capacity was available; in other instances, imports were automatically prohibited once domestic production began; in yet other cases, exceptionally high tariff walls, with levels reaching several hundreds of percentage points, effectively precluded all imports.

A number of difficulties gradually emerged with the import substitution strategy: export earnings rose even more slowly than might have been expected on the basis of the primary commodity composition of exports; exchange rates became increasingly unrealistic as authorities struggled to keep foreign exchange "cheap" in order to encourage domestic investment (which was thought to consist almost entirely of imported capital goods); and the rate at which import substitution could continue was constantly diminishing as "foreign exchange shortages" led to periodic balance-of-payments crises.

This is not the place to examine the difficulties of import substitution regimes.[14] Although analysts differ to some degree in their diagnosis of why these regimes yielded declining rates of economic growth, they all agree that there was a serious slowing down in growth rates in countries that had adopted and maintained import substitution policies. What does require comment, however, is the extent to which developing countries, by adopting highly protective trade policies, cut themselves off from the international economy. Table 1 shows that exports of developing countries (oil exporters excluded) rose much less rapidly than did industrial countries' exports during the 1950s and 1960s. Their share of world exports consequently fell from 32.6 percent in 1950 to 18 percent by 1970.

By the 1960s, however, a few developing countries were already changing their trade policies. The important point to note is that those countries which abandoned high walls of domestic protection as a way to encourage domestic industry, and turned instead to outer-oriented trade strategies, achieved exceptionally high rates of economic growth that had previously been regarded as unattainable. They experienced phenomenal rates of growth of manufactured exports, and with it, growth rates of real income in excess of 10 percent annually. Providing strong incentives for exports, these countries experienced growth of manufactured exports, primarily of labor-intensive products, at annual rates of 25, 30, and even 40 percent for several decades.

In so doing, they demonstrated that very rapid growth was indeed attainable if a country could provide the infrastructural investments, education, and incentives for individuals to follow the country's comparative advantage in the international market. Korea, one of the most spectacular of the outer-oriented countries, experienced real growth of output in excess of 10 percent annually for the entire period from 1960 to 1987, with exports rising from $33 million in 1960 to just over $30 billion in 1985.[15]

Thus, just as the international economy was faltering in the early 1980s, evidence became overwhelming that developing countries could, in a healthy international economic environment, grow very rapidly through reliance on the international market. Even countries adopting highly restrictionist and protectionist trade policies grow somewhat more rapidly when the world economy is exhibiting healthy growth than they do when it is more stagnant, but the biggest gains from a healthy, growing international economy accrue to those countries whose own policies are conducive to growth and to reliance on the international market.

During the worldwide recession of the early 1980s, many developing countries encountered major difficulties with their economies and with debt-servicing. Partly because the international economic environment was harsher than it had been a decade earlier, many developing countries experienced stagnant or even falling levels of per capita incomes in the early 1980s. In many instances, policies were reformed in an effort to restore growth—trade policies among them.

How much success will result from policy reforms will depend in part on the conviction with which domestic policymakers carry out the necessary changes, and in part on the openness of the international economy and its future growth. It is for this reason that the future course of the international economy is so vital to the prospects of the developing countries.[16]

The Uruguay Round of Trade Negotiations

The success of the outer-oriented developing countries has substantially increased their share of world trade, and made them major buyers and suppliers of a number of commodities. Their participation in future international trade negotiations is thus doubly important, for not only are they now important actors with a major stake in the system (and, in some cases, with major protectionist barriers still to dismantle), but their own economic futures depend in large part on the success of measures designed to resume the momentum of trade liberalization that characterized the period between 1950 and 1973.

For other developing countries, the issues are equally critical. The effectiveness of their policy reforms will be seriously reduced should the international economy fail to resume satisfactory growth. Meanwhile, many existing trade barriers are aimed at commodities of special interest to various developing countries: clothing and textiles are subject to the highly restrictive Multi-Fibre Arrangement; some temperate agricultural commodities are subject not only to restrictions on imports on the part of the United States, Japan, and the countries of the European Community (EC), but also to export subsidies in some instances.

As for the developed countries, a number of issues of central concern focus on barriers to entry of their exports into markets in developing countries. Whereas earlier rounds of trade negotiations could take place with developing countries passively benefitting from negotiations among the developed countries, many of the issues arising in the current environment involve the developing countries in central ways.

Thus, when alarmed authorities in the major trading countries began to consider the possibility of a new round of trade negotiations, it became clear that the developing countries' involvement would need to be at a different level of intensity than was earlier the case. This was exemplified by the name of the round itself: the "Uruguay Round" of trade negotiations was officially launched in Montevideo, Uruguay, in late 1986.

Scheduled to take place over several years, the hope is that the new Round can obtain agreement on a number of key issues affecting the international trading system: trade in agricultural commodities, trade in services, and agreements on a number of contentious issues—in the form of nontariff barriers—affecting trade in manufactures.[17]

The initial meeting in Montevideo was successful to a degree that was unanticipated: trade in agriculture was to be included on the agenda. This in itself represented a breakthrough, given the resistance of the Japanese and the European Community to such a step. But, in addition, the breakthrough came about because 14 agricultural exporting countries reached agreement among themselves to cooperate to insure the result. This represented the first concrete instance of a larger group of countries effectively cooperating to improve their bargaining power.

The degree and extent to which developing countries will participate in the Uruguay Round is still uncertain. Some developing countries actively opposed the new Round, arguing that developed countries actively discriminate against their exports and that they should first remove that discrimination before considering further measures. Others, however, actively support the new Round and intend to do their utmost to reduce barriers against their exports and to improve market access.

Nonetheless, it is clear that the major issue for the developing countries is the future path of the international economy. Should the volume of international trade grow at a rate of 5 to 6 percent annually—less than the rates of the 1950s and 1960s, but substantially above the rates of the early 1980s—the prospects for developing countries' abilities to resume satisfactory rates of growth would be reasonably sanguine. If, however, the negotiations falter and protectionist tendencies are strengthened, the difficulties of attaining satisfactory growth rates would increase inordinately.

Within the context of a satisfactory outcome, a number of issues will arise whose resolution will affect the developing countries. Much will depend on the understanding of those issues on the part of developing countries' representatives, and on the part of others concerned with developing countries' growth prospects.

Although the chapters in this volume are concerned with both sets of issues, their focus is largely on the issues of particular concern to developing countries. This is not because the overriding issues are not more important, but because they are being extensively dealt with elsewhere. Issues of concern to developing countries have not received much systematic attention, and yet they may be equally crucial to the outcome of the Uruguay Round.

The first paper, by D. Gale Johnson, focuses on prospects for improving the efficiency of world production and trade in agricultural commodities. Here, the central issue is the domestic policies of the major industrial countries, which are said to be designed to protect farmers' incomes, but which in fact fail to do so. Johnson analyzes alternative mechanisms by which agricultural production and trade could be liberalized in the interests of the developed and developing countries alike.[18] The necessary adjustments would be far less painful if the industrial countries could agree simultaneously to undertake liberalization. While such a liberalization would clearly benefit the industrial countries greatly, it would also improve the fortunes of those developing countries that are exporters of agricultural commodities.

The second paper, by Robert Baldwin, focuses on issues in trade in manufactures that are of special importance for developing countries. Baldwin notes that the alternative to multilateral resolution of issues for the developing countries is bilateral bargaining, and points out that the developing countries' interests will almost surely be better represented in a multilateral forum. A natural corollary is that developing countries must be much more active in the Uruguay Round than in past rounds, and that they must be prepared to make some concessions with regard to their own protective structures. He also focuses on GATT rules on Safeguard Actions, Subsidies, and Dumping, which he believes must be resolved if developing countries' market access to developed countries is to be improved.

The final paper, by David Finch and Constantine Michalopoulos, focuses on the relationship between the GATT, the World Bank, and the IMF. They too question the value of S&D and focus on the possibility of forming coalitions among developing countries on issues of common interest. They also look for ways in which the GATT itself could be strengthened, whereby the GATT review processes could highlight instances of protection, noting that small countries will gain the greater the role of multilateral agencies.

The discussants comment on each chapter, and the major discussions from the floor are reported at the end of each paper. Thereafter, a final chapter pulls together the major issues of interest from the viewpoint of the developing countries.

Policy Options and Liberalizing Trade in Agricultural Products: Addressing the Interests of Developing Countries

Introduction

There is no group of countries that has greater interest in the outcome of the current international efforts to liberalize trade in agricultural products than the 37 low-income countries with per capita incomes of less than $400 in 1985. This group of countries has a population of 2.4 billion or 46 percent of the world's population. Because agriculture is of such great importance in their economies, employing 72 percent of their labor and producing 32 percent of their gross domestic product, access to international markets on a liberal basis is very important to their welfare. Liberalization of trade is also important to both urban and rural consumers by providing superior alternatives for achieving reasonable stability of prices and supplies compared to many national measures now common in these countries.

In the low-income countries, agriculture remains as a major source of exports, though a rapidly declining one. In 1982-84 agricultural exports accounted for nearly one-third of all exports from low-income countries, down from nearly three-fifths between 1964 and 1966 (World Bank 1986, 3). In low-income Africa, farm exports still accounted for 68 percent of all exports from 1982 to 1984. These percentages of total exports may be compared with agriculture's 14 percent share in the industrial market economies.

Given the current governmental interventions in agricultural trade, one rather obvious consequence of a successful liberalization of trade in the current Round of negotiations in the General Agreement on Tariffs and Trade (GATT) would be to increase the agricultural exports of the low-income countries and to reduce the exports of the industrial countries. The declining trend in the relative importance of agricultural exports in the total exports of the low-income countries would be halted and perhaps reversed as a result of more favorable competitive conditions in export markets and improved access to markets in the industrial countries.

I shall first discuss some of the important conditions that exist that will have a major influence upon the trade negotiations for agriculture. The GATT rules that provide exceptions for agriculture to general GATT principles supporting liberal trade are an important part of the conditions that will influence the negotiations. Another major influence is the existence of substantial excess capacity in the agricultures of the industrial countries, which resulted in restraints on imports and subsidies on exports. I shall then consider what effects trade liberalization would have upon international prices of farm products. The argument then shows that farm people have very little to gain from agricultural protection, either in terms of the level of their incomes or stability. The concluding sections consider how market access for the less developed countries

(LDCs) could be achieved, a brief assessment of alternatives to trade liberalization, and a discussion of the limited value of preference for the exports of developing countries.

Precursors to Negotiations

The forthcoming GATT negotiations on agricultural trade start from a particular setting. This setting has many features, some negative and some positive. Let us begin with the negative ones. First, the GATT articles dealing with crucial trade measures—import barriers other than tariffs and export subsidies—are ambiguous and have for so long been ignored as to be largely meaningless. Second, the continued U.S. adherence to Section 22 of the Agricultural Adjustment Act of 1933 potentially makes a mockery of any trade negotiation that we conclude.[1] In particular, the continued retention of the GATT waiver obtained by the United States in 1955 that permitted the use of quantitative restrictions on imports in violation of Article XI means that our position in the negotiations is greatly weakened.[2] Third, policymakers in the European Community (EC) continue to accept the view that the Common Agricultural Policy (CAP) is either (a) not subject to negotiation or (b) consistent with GATT principles. Fourth, the Japanese government continues to emphasize to its people that the current features of their food policy are absolutely essential to the continued security and stability of Japan without presenting alternative means by which food security could be achieved at the same or lower cost to consumers and taxpayers when, in fact, most of the reasons for continuation of highly protectionist policies is based in domestic partisan politics.

Equally important as a barrier to successful negotiations is the belief by policymakers in the large industrial nations that the incomes of farm people depend primarily upon the level of farm output prices and that if farm output prices decline significantly, their farmers and farming communities would suffer irreparable damage. This view is so widely held in numerous capitals that it is perhaps the strongest single barrier to successful trade negotiations. While the U.S. bargaining proposal that has been put forward for the negotiations is to eliminate within a decade all subsidies and price interventions that have a significant effect upon production, marketing, and trade, there has been no effort to provide the background information and analysis that would help to gain support for the proposal among farmers and their political representatives in the United States, Western Europe, or Japan. Until there is a general agreement that high price supports are ineffective in increasing the returns to the labor and capital of farm families, there will continue to be great and perhaps insurmountable opposition to significant reduction of incentives for agricultural production.

It is harder to find positive characteristics of the landscape, though there are some. Four are worthy of note. First, there was the declaration in Tokyo by the heads of seven governments that it is important to the citizens of their countries that agricultural trade be liberalized. This was followed by the Ministerial Declaration at the Uruguay Round in September 1986 which included the following:

> The CONTRACTING PARTIES agree that there is an urgent need to bring more discipline and predictability to world agricultural trade by correcting and preventing restrictions and distortions, including those related to structural surpluses, so as to reduce the uncertainty, imbalances and instability in world agricultural markets. Negotiations shall aim to achieve greater liberalization of trade in agriculture and bring all measures affecting import access and export competition under strengthened and more operationally effective GATT rules and disciplines. . . .

The third positive element is the existence of the Cairns Group. If this group of important agricultural producers, including Argentina, Australia, Brazil, Canada, and Thailand, as well as several other exporters, can maintain a consistent position of full support for trade liberalization in agricultural products, they can bring a significant amount of pressure to bear upon those countries that maintain widespread trade interventions that limit imports, encourage production, discourage consumption, and lead to large amounts of uneconomic exports. It will take a very concerted effort; the political skins that enclose the agricultural interventions in Western Europe, the United States, and Japan are not easily penetrated. It is difficult to know whether one is being heard, let alone whether there is any likelihood of a positive response.

Fourth, over the past several years a substantial body of evidence has been created concerning the effects of national policies of income and price support upon the level and instability of international market prices, the costs to consumers and taxpayers, and the size of the transfers involved in these programs. This is in sharp contrast to the amount of published and public information available at the time of the Tokyo Round. Furthermore, some of the work has now been done by organizations that are paid for by governments or by international agencies. In particular I refer to the work presented in the World Bank's *World Development Report 1986* (1986) and the OECD report *National Policies and Agricultural Trade* (1987). I would also include in this group Geoff Miller's *The Political Economy of International Agricultural Policy Reform* (1986), since it clearly has the support of the government of Australia, and it probably provides a great deal of the impetus for the Cairns Group. There was a substantial amount of background work for the World Bank report, especially that of the Australians, Tyers and Anderson, and the efforts of the International Institute of Applied Systems Analysis. Note may also be taken of the report published by the Trilateral Commission, *Agricultural Policy and Trade: Adjusting Domestic Programs in an International Framework* (1985), authored by three individuals (of which I was one), from North America, Japan, and the European Community.

In recent years there has also been a much greater availability of scholarly books, monographs and articles that detail the high costs and ineffectiveness of Japanese, North American, and European Community farm programs compared to the number of studies available in the early and mid-1970s. There has also been more attention given to the reasons that agricultural protection has arisen and persists. Particular note should be taken of *The Political Economy of Agricultural Protection* (1986), by Kym Anderson and

Yujiro Hayami. This excellent book is only one, albeit a very important one, contribution to the research and writing on why agricultural protection has such staying power in the face of incontrovert-
ible evidence of high costs and limited success in achieving stated
objectives. There are also authoritative studies of possible negotiating strategies for the GATT negotiations on agriculture sponsored
by organizations of considerable standing. I refer to Dale Hathaway's *Agriculture and the GATT: Rewriting the Rules* (1987), a
study sponsored by the Institute for International Economics, and
Robert L. Paarlberg's *Fixing Farm Trade: Policy Options for the
United States* (1988), a study sponsored by the New York Council
on Foreign Relations.

Reference must also be made to the work sponsored by the
International Food Policy Research Institute and undertaken by
Alberto Valdes and Joachim Zietz. The first such publication was
*Agricultural Protection in the OECD Countries: Its Cost to Less
Developed Countries* (1980). There have been subsequent updates
and extensions by its authors. As the title of the monograph indicates, the studies measured the impact of agricultural price and
income support policies of the OECD countries upon trade opportunities for developing countries. To the best of my knowledge
there has been no recognition by notice of government officials in
countries with restrictive trade policies, and certainly not by modifi-
cation of the policies that have such negative consequences for
developing countries. It cannot be said that there have been no
opportunities for either notice or policy reform since it was made
clear what some of the negative consequences have been for farm
people in some of the poorest countries in the world. In fact, agricultural protection affecting the exports of LDCs has increased
since 1980 rather than diminished.

Excess Capacity: A Major Barrier to Policy Reform

An important reason that negotiations for reduction of agricultural
protection by OECD countries presents such intractable problems

is that the protective measures have resulted in the creation of significant excess agricultural capacity. The capacity is excess not only for the industrial market economies but for the world as a whole. It is simply not acceptable for policymakers in OECD countries to use the existence of an unknown, though undoubtedly significant, number of malnourished people in the developing countries as a rationale for continuing to encourage agricultural production.

The existence of excess capacity in world agriculture is a major barrier to successful agricultural trade negotiations. It could be argued that the most important barrier to successful negotiations is the loss of income to farm families due to the reduction of the income transfers associated with the protective devices. But the income transfers have only a modest effect upon the incomes of farm families. There are several reasons for this; two are noted here. One is that a large fraction of the transfers do not go directly, or even very indirectly, to farmers but instead pay for storage, administration, interest cost on stockholdings, and spoilage or deterioration of products in storage. In the United States in 1985 and 1986 combined, less than $20 billion out of total governmental costs of more than $50 billion went directly to farmers in the form of diversion, deficiency, and storage payment. A part of this amount, namely that for diversion and storage, did not go directly to net income. True, some of the program effects resulted in higher farm prices, especially in the case of dairy products, peanuts, and sugar. But even in these instances the amount translated into net farm income was much less than the gross transfer from consumers. Furthermore, if it were not for the excess capacity that has been generated, the market prices for farm products would be higher than they now are in many instances.

A similar pattern of government expenditures on agricultural programs exists in the European Community. Of total EC expenditures in 1986, about two-fifths went for export subsidies and half that much for storage. The remainder went for various costs of maintaining price supports at high levels: denaturing of wheat for feed use or disposal of butter and dry skim milk as feed (USDA 1987, 36-37).

Excess Agricultural Capacity. All developed market economies have had government agricultural policies that have created excess capacity. What do I mean by excess capacity? It is perhaps easier to define what I mean by reference to excess resources. Excess resources are quantities of resources greater than those that could earn a return in agriculture comparable to what similar resources earn in the rest of the economy, when the prices received and paid by farmers are those prevailing in a world free-trade regime. Resources used in agriculture are assumed to be fully employed, though not necessarily in agriculture. Some resources, especially labor, may find their best and most profitable use by combining work in agriculture and some other activity.

The excess resources, of course, have the capacity to create excess supply. This capacity may or may not be realized in full. In the EC generally and in the U.S. dairy industry until quite recently, the excess resources were induced to produce an excess supply. For several crop products, the United States has engaged in supply management through limiting the quantity of one input—land— that could be devoted to production. In recent years the EC has utilized output quotas for dairy and sugar to reduce excess supply.

It is worth making clear the difference between excess resources and excess supply. Excess supply can be eliminated by a government supply management program that results in an output that can be sold at the prevailing prices or, if one wishes to use the same approach as used in defining excess resources, at the prices that would prevail in a free-trade world. But what has to be emphasized is that eliminating excess supply by output quotas or input limitations does not result in the elimination of excess capacity. The capacity to produce is not reduced by such governmental programs. Once the restraints, whether an output quota or an input limitation, are removed, and if the same price incentives are maintained, the excess resources are transformed into excess supply.

Two implications may be noted. One is that an input limitation, such as used in U.S. supply management programs, may actually result in adding to the excess resources. This occurs because when land use is limited, the demand for other resources that are close substitutes for land increases. These include short-run responses, such as added fertilizer and pesticide and herbicide inputs, which presumably would be withdrawn when the land input is no longer rationed, but probably not instantaneously. The response also includes some long-lived investments, such as drainage and irrigation, that add to productive capacity in the long run. There are some offsetting reductions in resource demand due to limiting the land input. Inputs such as labor that have a low elasticity of substitution with land will be reduced when the land input is reduced. Quite possibly the same may be true of machinery, but perhaps not. When the land input is artificially reduced, the value of timeliness of field operations may increase, and this may induce farmers to maintain approximately the same stock of machinery even for the reduced area.

The other implication refers to the longer run effects of a program, such as the U.S. dairy herd buyout. In the short run, it seems to be effective in reducing both excess resources and excess supply. But unless there are decreasing returns to scale of farms in milk production, it is reasonable to assume that the reduction both in excess resources and excess supply will be temporary. Dairy cows can be replaced rather quickly when the forced reduction in numbers is less than 10 percent. And existing farmers can bring together the other resources that were either temporarily or permanently withdrawn from dairy production as a consequence of the operators' five-year commitment to stay out of dairy production in return for participating in the dairy herd buyout. Thus the effects of such an effort on either excess resources or supply will be short lived. It has merit only if sufficient adjustment is made in price incentives to prevent the resources that were withdrawn from being replaced.

Limiting Excess Supply with Excess Resources. When does it make economic sense to limit excess supply when excess resources exist? Only when the current market situation is a temporarily depressed one. In other words, if output prices are now low and there is near certainty that prices will soon return to a higher and more normal level, a temporary effort to limit excess supply may be both politically and economically acceptable. Such effort to limit current excess supply may be an acceptable alternative when past policy errors have resulted in the creation of enormous inventories of storable products, including some such as butter that are only storable at reasonable cost for a limited period of time. These two circumstances are related, of course. Excess supply may be transformed into inventory stocks rather than sold into the market, thereby further depressing current prices. After any expectation that current prices are about to recover to acceptable levels and if stocks have grown to unacceptable levels, efforts to limit supply even in the face of continued excess resources may be an acceptable alternative to provide for time to achieve resource adjustment.

Efforts to reduce excess supply, while doing nothing to achieve resource adjustment, have no historical precedent to support their effectiveness in improving the long-run viability of agriculture. After all, the major piece of U.S. farm legislation that has been the intellectual basis for all subsequent legislation for more than a half century was called the Agricultural Adjustment Act of 1933. It was designed to deal with the emergency conditions created jointly by the Great Depression of the 1930s and large stocks of farm commodities. Similarly the Payment-In-Kind (PIK) program in 1983 was to deal with an emergency situation caused by several factors, including a slowdown of demand growth in international markets and a loss in U.S. market share culminating in large stocks owned by the CCC.[3] But the solution to that emergency turned out to be short-lived in its effects: prices improved temporarily but then continued at low and declining levels, and by 1985 stocks were as large as at the beginning of 1983.

The price and income policies of North America, Western Europe, and Japan have had some limited effect in reducing excess supplies, but these policies have not eliminated excess resources.

The high governmental costs incurred by all three nations for their farm policies indicate that excess resources remain. The Japanese are able to equate supply and demand for rice, after a fashion, with high producer prices, and subsidized consumer prices and large payments for diversion of land. The EC has almost eliminated the excess supply of sugar, but given the high producer prices for production no one can reasonably claim that the excess resources have been eliminated. Even if the United States were to eliminate excess supply of grains and cotton in 1988 or 1989, it would still be saddled with annual governmental costs of $15-$20 billion.

The annual taxpayer and consumer costs incurred in the industrial economies are a rough approximation of what it costs to maintain excess resources in agriculture. For the early 1980s, Tyers and Anderson (1987, 49) estimate that, in terms of 1985 U.S. dollars, the combined consumer and taxpayer costs were about $60 billion in the EC, $30 billion in Japan, and $20 billion in the United States. Levels of protection were much lower from 1980 to 1982 than today. Even so, these costs were large compared to net farm operator incomes in the early 1980s. Rough estimates of net farm operator income from 1980 to 1982 averaged $40 billion in the EC-10. For the United States the average was $22 billion, for Japan it was $20 billion. These figures should be adjusted upward by about 10 percent to convert into 1985 U.S. dollars. Thus the cost of retaining excess resources in agriculture was equal to or greater than net farm operator income in the three comparisons.

One reason for the high cost of transferring income to farmers under the circumstances that prevail in Western Europe, Japan, and the United States is that farmer-supplied inputs have now become a minority of the inputs used in agriculture production. A large part of the transfer—the cost of excess resources in agriculture—goes to pull resources from the nonfarm economy into agriculture. While directly comparable data are not available, the share of intermediate consumption—basically current inputs of nonfarm origin—as defined by OECD were the following approximate percentages of the value of farm production in the early 1980s:

EC-10   50%
Japan   42%
U.S.   47%

Consequently only a part of the costs imposed upon consumers and taxpayers by the farm price and income policies of the industrial economies goes to the farmer-supplied inputs of labor, management, and land. The earlier comparison of the transfer costs and net farm operator incomes exaggerate the proportion of the transfers retained in agriculture. The reason is that in each of the areas there are major components of agriculture that receive little or no protection under existing policies. This is the case in the United States for all livestock production, except dairy, and for a considerable number of crops other than grain and cotton. In the EC many livestock farmers also receive little benefit from the CAP and the same is true for certain fruit and vegetable producers in Japan.

The share of intermediate consumption in total farm output fails to reflect the full significance of nonfarm inputs as sources of output expansion and claimants upon the income produced in agriculture. In the United States the net returns to farm land, owned capital, all labor and management was approximately a quarter of farm output even if one subtracts all expenditures upon livestock and feed from the measure of gross output. Similar calculations for four EC members (Denmark, Germany, United Kingdom, and France) indicate that the returns to resources enumerated above as a percentage of farm output range from 18 percent in Denmark to 36 percent in France. Consequently, if all inputs of nonfarm origin are included—capital items as well as current inputs—such inputs account for between 65 and 80 percent of total inputs used in agricultural production. Over a period of a decade, the elasticity of supply of these nonfarm inputs approach infinity.[4]

How Many Excess Resources? Few efforts have been made to measure the quantity of excess resources in agriculture. There were some attempts made by the United States during the late 1960s and early 1970s. The measures were based primarily upon the amount of land diverted, with differences in the estimates depending upon the evaluation of the probable product of the diverted land. Estimates of excess productive capacity included those made by Tweeten and Quance (1972), Tyner and Tweeten (1964), and another by Mayer, Heady, and Madsen (1968).

At the time I argued that the first two estimates were too large, primarily because much of the diverted land was unlikely to return to crop cultivation even if the supply management programs were ended (Johnson 1973). In other words, much of the land that was diverted from 1970 to 1972 was only useful for "farming" the farm programs and not for growing corn, wheat, or cotton. In 1972, for example, the amount of land diverted under the wheat, feed grains, and cotton programs was 59 million acres. In 1974, when there were no acreage limitations, the acreage planted of wheat, feed grain, cotton, and soybeans was 28 million acres more than in 1972. The returned acreage was just 47 percent of what the farm programs had made diversion payments on two years earlier. True, two years later the increase in planted area over 1972 was equal to two-thirds of the area diverted in 1972. But there is considerable evidence that a significant part of the increase in planted area by 1976, and even further increases later, was due to development of new cropland, rather than the return of all the diverted land. In a 1973 study I estimated that the excess resources in U.S. agriculture had been reduced to 2 percent by 1972. Nearly all of this was concentrated in crop production and, specifically, in wheat, feed grains, and cotton. Mayer, Heady, and Madsen (1968) estimated that supply management reduced aggregate farm output by approximately 2 percent in the early 1970s.

My view that there were few excess resources in U.S. agriculture in the early 1970s has been contested on the ground that the government expenditures on farm programs, measured in constant prices, were as large during 1970 and 1972 as during the early 1960s. In terms of 1982 dollars, average annual government expenditures from 1970 to 1972 were $9.6 billion compared to $10.3 billion from 1962 to 1965. However, during the early

1970s, feed grain stocks were being reduced and the dollar was overvalued, probably by 10 percent. The overvaluation of the dollar did not just happen in the early 1970s, but had existed for a number of years. This overvaluation clearly depressed gross farm income and would have resulted in fewer resources being engaged in agriculture than would have been true in a free-trade world. The government farm programs, with the deficiency payments and price supports above market-clearing levels, held more resources in agriculture than could have been sustained at market-clearing prices, given the overvaluation of the dollar. Thus, during these early 1970s, there were excess supplies at the then prevailing prices, but there were relatively few excess resources.

A recent study by Dvoskin (1988, 5) of the U.S. Department of Agriculture (USDA) estimates the amount of excess capacity or resources in U.S. agriculture for the years from 1940 to date. He measures excess capacity as the sum of commodities acquired under the farm price support programs, the value of noncommercial or subsidized exports, and the value of production potential from set-aside or diverted cropland. This recent study confirms my estimate that the degree of excess capacity in the early 1970s was just 2 percent, but the study also estimates that the excess capacity in 1986 had increased by fourfold—to 8 percent. Thus the agricultural policies since the mid-1970s failed to continue the progress toward market orientation that was accomplished from the mid-1950s through the early 1970s. Instead, the policies encouraged the reemergence of substantial excess capacity. In fact, the measure of excess capacity for the mid-1980s was substantially above the earlier peak level reached in the mid-1960s. The excess capacity is concentrated in wheat, feed grains, cotton, and dairy—commodities which have price supports. Farm products, especially the meat animals, that do not have a price support program are not subject to long-run excess productive capacity.

Another approach, and probably a preferable one, to estimate excess resources in agriculture has been utilized by Andy Stoeckel and associates for the EC-10 (Brechling 1987). A general equilibrium model was estimated. Two critical parameters were a long-run elasticity of agricultural supply of 0.3 and price enhancement by the Common Agricultural Policy of 50 percent from the mid-1970s to the early 1980s. On the basis of these and other assumptions, it was estimated that EC agricultural output had been increased 18 percent by the CAP. According to this estimate, approximately half the increase in EC agricultural output during the past two decades has been generated by the CAP. Or if applied specifically to grain, it means that in the 1980s, the European Community would have been a net importer of perhaps 20 million tons of grain, approximately its position 15 years earlier.

One can quarrel with some of the assumptions. Perhaps the long-run aggregate supply elasticity of 0.3 is too high, but if you reduce it by one-third, there is still an output increase of 12 percent. On the other hand, the price enhancement offered by the CAP probably averaged more than 50 percent over the past two decades. While output may have been increased by 18 percent by CAP compared to what it would have been under free trade, this estimate undervalues the impact of the CAP on world trade in farm products since an important impact of the CAP prices has been to reduce consumption in the EC. Should the 18 percent output increase be adjusted downward to account for the increased consumption that would occur in the EC under free trade? Only to a limited degree, since the increase in EC consumption would then be a factor affecting world demand and prices and thus the equilibrium level of agricultural output in the EC. If world market prices increased by 15 percent, as estimated by Tyers and Anderson (1987), from 1980 through 1982, the long-run effect would be to increase EC agricultural output by about 4.5 percent. Thus if all industrial market economies liberalized their agricultural trade, EC excess agricultural resources might be put at about 13 to 14 percent of the level of resource use from 1980 to 1982.

There are substantial excess resources in Japanese agriculture. The combination of tax treatment of agricultural land and the restrictions imposed upon the sale and leasing of land make it difficult to estimate how many excess resources would be in agriculture if there were both free trade and freedom to buy, sell, and transfer land without governmental intervention.[5] It seems idle to speculate about the degree of excess resources now in agriculture as it is highly probable that trade liberalization would be followed by domestic liberalization in the use of agricultural resources. With this rationalization, Japanese agriculture output would be reduced by far less than the relative quantity of resources removed from agriculture due to the significant improvements in productivity. While the excess resources in EC agriculture are generally efficiently used in a technological sense, such is not the case in Japan.

Supply management that resolved an excess supply situation could be an appropriate second-best policy if it were correctly assumed that the causes of the disequilibrium between supply and demand at the price objective (target or threshold price) were temporary in nature or that there was some reasonable expectation of changing conditions resulting in significantly higher prices. Is there any reasonable chance that the present concern about excess resources in agriculture in the United States is misplaced?

It is true that current international prices of grains and soybeans are exceedingly low in real terms. Real grain prices are below those of the Great Depression and significantly below the trend line for the past six decades. In real terms, U.S. export prices of wheat in late 1987 were about 25 percent, or $15 per ton (in 1967 dollars), below the long-term trend (1925-29 to 1983-85), and corn was almost 40 percent below the trend value. The low level of prices is due to some considerable extent to the U.S. effort to dispose of stocks accumulated as the result of prior high price supports and high target prices. If and when the stocks return to more normal levels, market prices will increase. But there is little reason to expect the recovery to raise grain prices above their long-term trend values.

True, in addition to the depressing effect of U.S. disposal operations, current international prices are depressed as a result of slow world economic growth and the import restraints imposed by heavily indebted developing countries. Thus, sooner or later, international prices will strengthen relative to recent levels but will not be likely to rise above trend levels.

There can be little doubt that international market prices for grains and soybeans will increase from the current very low levels over the next few years. How much the prices will recover depends upon the pace of world economic growth, the degree of resolution of LDC debt problems, and the reduction of incentives for the production of agricultural products in the industrial countries. Prices will remain significantly depressed until the ratio of world stocks to consumption for grains returns to more normal levels. But since it is always a mistake to believe things are really as good as they seem, it is equally wrong to assume that things are really as bad as they seem. Tomorrow will be brighter than today. But there is no foundation for the assumption that the price improvement that can be realistically anticipated will be great enough to employ the resources that are now engaged in U.S. agriculture at returns comparable to those available in the rest of the economy. Resources must exit from agriculture if U.S. agriculture is to receive its returns from the prices that prevail in the international market and not from the U.S. Treasury or by forcing U.S. consumers to pay in excess of world market prices for what they eat or wear. The same conclusion applies with at least equal force to the EC and the rest of Western Europe as well as to Japan.

Excess Resources Have Other Origins. While agricultural price and income policies bear much of the blame for the existence of excess resources in industrial country agricultures, there are other sources. Most of the excess resources now in U.S. agriculture are due to national and individual decisions made in the 1970s.

The substantial growth of investment in agriculture resulted from the macroeconomic policies that resulted in negative real interest rates for several years, federal income tax policies that made agriculture into an enormous tax shelter, and inaccurate expectations on the part of many farmers that the good times would continue to roll. These expectations were fueled by misleading statements emanating from Independence Avenue in Washington, culminating in a national disgrace, *The Global 2000 Report to the President*. The erroneous expectations infested the Congress and the Reagan Administration as evidenced by the 1981 Farm Bill, which seemed to be based on the assumption that world demand for food was going to outstrip supply for years to come.

It was not only in the United States that unrealistic expectations were held by both farmers and government officials. As late as 1983, Japanese officials continued to emphasize that world food shortages were highly likely. They have not as yet retracted their erroneous projections, (Johnson 1986). In its 1981 *Guidelines for European Agriculture*, the EC Commission justified high and stable prices on the grounds that European consumers could not be assured that they "could be supplied for long at low, stable prices if Community supply, because of reduction in production, would depend to a greater degree on imports" (Johnson 1986).

Elimination of Excess Capacity. The lengthy discussion of excess capacity and the underlying excess resources leads to a number of propositions that affect the policy options available in the efforts to reduce agricultural trade barriers. The first is that the extension of supply management programs to the EC and to other exporters of grains may reduce excess supplies to a level that is politically manageable; they will not reduce or eliminate excess agricultural resources in the industrial countries or in the world, or make possible a significant reduction in barriers to trade in farm products. If supply management is the wave of the future and resolves the conflicts between major industrial country exporters of agricultural products, there is little or no prospect for increases in agricultural exports by the developing countries.

The second proposition is that domestic agricultural policy reform designed to eliminate excess agricultural resources in the OECD is essential for agricultural trade liberalization. Unless such reforms are honestly and energetically addressed by OECD countries, especially the United States and the EC, we will witness further restrictions on agricultural trade rather than freer trade.

The third proposition is one that needs continuous repetition, namely that the possibility of any country eliminating excess agricultural resources will be greatly enhanced if all nations pursue such efforts simultaneously and international market prices gradually increase from their current depressed levels. Numerous studies of the effects of free trade on international market prices generally come to a common conclusion: with free trade, international market prices would increase for the grain, dairy, and livestock products. The prices of some products, particularly soybeans and manioc and corn gluten feed, whose demand has been artificially increased by trade policy measures would probably suffer price losses.

The fourth and last proposition is that political, economic, and social realities require that programs to eliminate excess resources be given an extended period of time to achieve their objectives. The economic and social dislocations to follow a "cold shower" approach of rapid abolition of existing programs are greater than the democratic process can tolerate for governments where there is no clear and definite majority by any political party. These expectations may be excessively pessimistic, but it is unlikely that any OECD democracy would risk rapid withdrawal of farm subsidies and high prices. New Zealand has already pursued such a policy. This provides an opportunity to follow and evaluate the effects upon farm income and output produced by the drastic reforms undertaken in that country. It takes great political courage to implement such a radical approach, and unfortunately, courage is not a commodity in excess supply—quite unlike many farm products.

International Price Effects of Trade Liberalization

If the industrial market economies had free trade in agricultural products, there would be two major effects upon international market prices. The effect that most attention is given to is that for almost all farm products, international market prices would be increased, and in some cases by very substantial percentages. An effect that policymakers tend to ignore is that international market prices would become much more stable. It is odd that this effect is so generally ignored since one of the prime objectives of agricultural price policy, especially in Western Europe and Japan, is to achieve price stability for their farmers. Perhaps the reason for their ignoring the positive contribution that free or liberal trade would make in reducing international price instability is that they do not wish to admit that they have been purchasing domestic farm price stability at the expense of others, especially of low-income farmers in developing countries.

No attempt will be made to summarize the results of all the studies that have been made of the effects of trade liberalization upon international market prices. At best, the results need to be interpreted with caution. Because of differences in time periods used for measuring degrees of protection and in assumptions made concerning basic parameters, such as elasticities of supply and demand, it is very difficult to compare the results of various studies. Thus differences in outcomes should not be unexpected. In particular there have been significant changes in the degrees of protection for the periods included in the various studies. Protection levels in the industrial market economies were relatively low in the mid-1970s and early 1980s. For the EC, protection levels between 1980 and 1982 were generally below those that prevailed during the late 1960s and early 1970s. In the United States, protection levels were quite low between 1980 and 1982 but increased sharply over the next two or three years while protection in the EC remained about the same as in the prior years. A USDA analysis of changes in producer subsidy equivalents (PSEs), a measure of protection levels, found that between 1979 and 1981, the PSE for the United States was 13 percent of the total value of agricultural output, compared to 33 percent for the EC; between 1982 and 1984, the U.S. PSE had increased to 22 percent, while the EC figure declined very slightly to 31 percent (USDA December 1987, 38). The decline in the European Community PSE was mainly due to the sharp rise in international market prices measured in ECUs, the monetary unit used in determining price guarantees in the EC. Whereas at the beginning of 1982 the

ECU and the dollar were at rough parity, by the end of 1984 the ECU had a value of approximately $0.70.

With the implementation of the Food Security Act of 1985, coincident with the fall in the foreign exchange value of the dollar, there have been sharp increases in the levels of agricultural protection in the industrial market economies. In early 1987, Tyers and Anderson projected what the levels of protection might be in 1988 and in 1995, based on existing agricultural policies and the projected trend in international market prices. They projected that continuation of existing policies would produce a decline in real international food prices of approximately 50 percent between 1980-82 and 1988. This projection, as of late 1987, seems to be reasonably accurate if the particular commodity mix is taken into account. Nominal grain prices have fallen by almost 50 percent and nominal sugar prices by more than 50 percent. Table 1 is taken directly from Tyers and Anderson. It shows for all industrial market economies an increase in nominal protection from 1.40 from 1980 through 1982 to a projected 2.00 for 1988 with some decline to 1.80 by 1995 as international market prices are projected to recover somewhat even with a continuation of existing farm price and income policies. The projections in Table 1 indicate the importance of a positive result from the Uruguay Round negotiations. If there are no negotiations or no positive results, levels of protection in the 1990s are likely to be higher than in the early 1980s and not very much different from the high levels of 1988. This is a result that would bode ill for the developing countries of the world.

Table 2 is taken from a 1987 revision of work Tyers and Anderson did for the *World Development Report 1986*. The first part of the table presents projections of international price and trade effects, assuming 1980-82 levels of protection, compared to what would have been the case had trade been liberalized by certain countries or groups of countries. The price effects, shown in the top part of Table 2, are projections of the effect of actual trade interventions compared to what would have existed had there been free trade for an extended period of time. For example, the protec-

Table 1

Producer-to-Border Price Ratios, Various Commodities and Industrial Market
Economies, Estimated 1980–92 and Projected 1988 and 1995[a]

	Wheat	Coarse Grain	Rice	Ruminant Meat	Non-ruminant Meat	Dairy Products	Sugar	Weighted Average (GLS)[b]
EC-12								
1980–82	1.40	1.40	1.35	1.95	1.25	1.75	1.50	1.55
1988	3.40	2.40	2.40	2.75	1.60	2.50	2.80	2.25
1995	2.60	1.75	2.20	2.50	1.35	2.50	3.00	2.05
EFTA-5								
1980–82	1.65	1.55	1.00	2.30	1.40	2.45	1.55	1.90
1988	3.90	2.85	1.00	4.25	1.90	3.90	3.20	3.15
1995	2.05	1.55	1.00	4.35	1.65	4.40	3.90	3.35
Japan								
1980–82	3.90	4.30	3.35	2.80	1.50	2.90	3.00	2.35
1988	8.00	11.65	8.20	5.40	1.90	5.55	7.10	3.80
1995	3.90	9.30	9.30	5.15	1.90	6.45	8.55	3.65
United States								
1980–82	1.15	1.00	1.30	1.10	1.00	2.00	1.40	1.20
1988	2.20	1.60	1.85	1.30	1.00	2.20	2.05	1.50
1995	1.30	1.00	1.60	1.30	1.00	2.30	1.95	1.25
All Industrial Market Economies								
1980–82	1.25	1.15	2.50	1.50	1.20	1.90	1.50	1.40
1988	2.45	1.75	5.65	2.05	1.40	2.55	2.60	2.00
1995	1.75	1.20	6.15	1.95	1.30	2.70	2.80	1.80

Source: Table 7 and GLS Model projections. Rod Tyers and Kym Anderson, "Global Interactions and Trade Liberalization in Agriculture," World Bank unpublished paper. Revised April 1987, 60.

[a]The projected ratios are taken from the reference projection described in the text. A ratio of 1.00 indicates the absence of protection.

[b]GLS refers to Grains, Livestock products, and Sugar.

tionist policy of the EC-12 was to reduce the international market price of wheat by 6 percent and dairy products by 25 percent. Agricultural protection in all industrial market economies (IMEs) and LDCs was projected to have reduced international market prices for wheat by 10 percent and for dairy products by 41 percent from 1980 through 1982.

The second part of Table 2 shows the effects of protectionist policies upon international price instability. With the agricultural protection that existed between 1980 and 1982, the coefficient of variation of international wheat prices was estimated to be 58 percent (the standard deviation divided by the mean price). However, if there were free trade by all IMEs and LDCs, the variability would have been reduced by nearly four-fifths to 15 percent. These projections support the general conclusion that much of international price instability is due to acts of man and not of nature (Johnson 1974).

Table 3 presents Tyers and Anderson's projected effects of the degree of protection that prevailed in 1988 upon international market prices. Projections were made for the price effects of agricultural protection in all industrial market economies and for the EC-12 and the United States. Generally speaking, the long-run depressing effects upon international market prices of the 1988 protection levels was projected to be 2.5 times as great as the 1980-82 protection levels. Wheat prices would be depressed by 20 percent and dairy product prices by 47 percent in 1995.

The projections in Table 3 also indicate that in the short run the policies followed by the United States may increase world market prices. This result follows in part because of the stockholdings accumulated under current farm programs and the assumption that under trade liberalization such stocks would be liquidated. The modest long-run price effects are due to the credit given to the U.S. supply management programs for limiting U.S. production of grains. But as noted earlier, U.S. supply management programs do not eliminate excess resources in agriculture.

Farm People Gain Little from Protection

As noted earlier, a major obstacle to success in the negotiations is that there is so little understanding among national decision makers concerning the effectiveness of agricultural price and income programs in achieving their stated objectives. The avowed objectives of protectionism are to increase the incomes of farm people, to

Table 2

International Price and Trade Effects of Agricultural Protection in Industrial Market Economies (IMEs), 1980–82

	Wheat	Coarse Grain	Rice	Ruminant Meat	Non-ruminant Meat	Dairy Products	Sugar	All GLS[e]
International Price Level								
% difference due to policies in:								
EC-12	−6	−5	−3	−18	−4	−25	−7	−10
EFTA-5	−1	−1	−1	−3	0	−6	0	−1
Japan	−1	−1	−6	−5	−4	−10	−2	−3
All WE & EA[a]	−7	−6	−12	−23	−8	−31	−10	−12
United States	−1	4	0	−3	1	−22	−3	−4
All IMEs[b]	0	−3	−10	−21	−7	−38	−10	−14
All IMEs and LDCs[c]	−10	−2	8	−13	3	−41	1	−9
International Price Instability								
Reference coefficient of variation	.58	.53	.38	.24	.08	.26	.36	
Coefficient of variation in the absence of protection in:								
EC-12	.39	.45	.32	.15	.08	.13	.28	
Japan	.54	.51	.33	.09	.07	.18	.33	
All WE & EA[a]	.35	.41	.27	.08	.06	.11	.25	
United States	.60	.64	.36	.17	.10	.27	.31	
All IMEs[b]	.33	.47	.28	.07	.08	.11	.25	
All IMEs and LDCs[c]	.15	.23	.09	.04	.05	.06	.07	

World Trade Volume

% difference due to policies in:

EC-12	4	0	1	-58	6	-17	0
EFTA-5	0	-1	1	-10	-1	-12	0
Japan	0	3	-18	-22	-46	-29	-1
All WE & EA[a]	3	2	-22	-64	-54	-27	-2
United States	2	-11	3	-17	-9	-45	-3
All IMEs[b]	6	-9	-15	-63	-44	-39	-3
All IMEs and LDCs[c]	-1	-19	-48	-71	-84	-56	-39

Net Export Volume[d]

Million tonne difference due to all IME policies for:

All WE & EA[a]	4.5	4.0	3.8	5.6	1.7	14.0	2.3
Australasia & North America	0.0	-8.6	2.0	-2.1	-0.9	14.4	0.7
Centrally Planned Europe	-2.6	1.9	-0.0	-0.5	-0.0	-6.2	0.0
Other Developing Countries	-4.9	2.3	-4.0	-2.9	-0.7	-22.0	-2.9

Source: Table 7 and GLS Model projections. Rod Tyers and Kym Anderson, "Global Interactions and Trade Liberalization in Agriculture," World Bank unpublished paper. Revised April 1987, 42.

[a] All WE & EA refers to the Western European Countries in EC-12 and EFTA-5 plus the East Asian protectionist economies of Japan, Korea, and Taiwan. The 12 members of the EC are Belgium, Denmark, France, Germany FR, Greece, Ireland, Italy, Luxembourg, Netherlands, Portugal. Spain, and the United Kingdom. The five members of the European Free Trade Area are Austria, Finland, Norway, Sweden, and Switzerland.

[b] All IMEs refers to Western Europe and Japan (but not Korea and Taiwan) plus Australia, Canada, New Zealand, and the United States.

[c] GLS liberalization in developing countries as well as industrial market economies (that is, global GLS liberalization including Centrally Planned Europe).

[d] The extent to which exports are greater or imports are less as a result of agricultural protection in W. Europe and E. Asia. A negative sign signifies that those policies have reduced exports or increased imports for that group of countries.

[e] The index of all GLS prices is based on weights derived from the 1980–82 shares of each commodity group's exports in total GLS exports. GLS refers to Grains, Livestock products, and Sugar.

Table 3
International Price Effects of Agricultural Protection in Industrial Market
Economies 1988 and 1995
(Percent difference compared to prices under free trade)

Differences Due to 1988 Policies in:	Wheat	Coarse Grain	Rice	Ruminant Meat	Non-ruminant Meat	Dairy Products	Sugar	Weighted Average
EC-12								
1988–90	–19	–6	–7	–15	–4	–22	–6	–13
1995	–19	–5	–9	–21	–4	–37	–15	–18
United States								
1988–90	+22	+11	+15	+2	–4	–3	0	+11
1995	–2	+6	+1	–6	–2	–21	–3	–4
All Industrial Market Economies								
1988–90	+6	+2	0	–18	–4	–29	–7	–8
1995	–20	–3	–15	–30	–9	–47	–18	–23

Source: Rod Tyers and Kym Anderson, "Global Interactions and Trade Liberalization in Agriculture," World Bank unpublished paper. Revised April 1987, 13.

provide for food security, to maintain viable rural communities, and to achieve stability of farm incomes.

Increased Incomes. High prices or subsidies are presumed to increase the returns to farm labor and capital. But the presumption is without foundation except for the relative short run. True, if there is an increase in output prices, the incomes of farm operators will increase in that crop year. This will be true because revenue will increase, and there will be little or no change in output or costs. But let the higher price be maintained for a period of time and adjustments will occur that negate the effects upon returns to labor, management, and capital. The only resource owners that will gain are the owners of land. I know of no social or economic benefit resulting from higher land prices that justifies either higher prices to consumers or an increase in governmental expenditures. One can only wonder why decision makers do not understand that higher land prices mean that when new farmers enter agriculture they must pay existing land owners for the privilege to become farmers. In other words, existing owners of land reap the advantages of the higher prices. How much current owners gain will depend upon how large the price increase is and how long it is expected to prevail.

The incomes of farm people are determined hardly at all by farm income and price policies. What determines the return to farm labor and management are the returns to comparable persons in the rest of the economy. In other words, the incomes of farm people are determined primarily by the per capita incomes of the country in which they live.[6] Differences in average levels of farm prices have almost no effect upon the returns to farm labor and management. This might not have been true 50 years or so ago when many of today's farm programs were first put in place. At that time farm areas were not nearly as fully integrated into the rest of the economy as is true today. Improvements in communication (rural mail delivery, telephones, radios, and televisions) and in transportation (paved roads, automobiles, and rural buses) have removed most of the differences between farm and urban life and have substantially reduced the costs of transferring from farming to some other desired activity. The integration of farm and nonfarm activities has become so pervasive in the United States that approximately 70 percent of the income of farm operator families has come from nonfarm sources in recent years; in Canada, during the same period, half or more of the income of farm families has come from nonfarm sources. In Japan approximately four-fifths of the income of farm families is derived from off-farm sources, primarily employment income of one or more family members.

Given the much greater density of population, it is somewhat surprising that the importance of nonfarm income for farm families in the EC is less than it is in North America. Approximately one-third of all farms in the EC are part-time, a much lower percentage than in Canada or the United States.

It seems obvious from the integration of rural and urban life in most industrial countries that returns to mobile farm resources cannot long depart significantly from the returns to comparable resources in the rest of the economy. This is certainly true of investment resources. And it is also true of farm labor. With so many farm families combining farm and nonfarm work and with the potentials for migration as great as they are, farm earnings below nonfarm earnings will induce more farm people to shift to nonfarm jobs. If returns to farm labor exceed those that could be earned off the farm, it is not necessary that urban people move to the farm but only that the movement of labor out of agriculture slow down.

Those who expect that farm prices and income policies can have a significant permanent effect upon the return to farm labor apparently forget that in the industrial economies, farm employment declines year after year. The reasons for the decline in farm employment are primarily twofold. One is that the demand for farm products grows more slowly than the demand for nonfarm goods and services. The other reason is that labor productivity increases at least as fast in agriculture as in the rest of the economy—in fact, since World War II the growth of labor productivity in agriculture in OECD countries has been larger than in the rest of the economy. These two effects have resulted in farm employment declining generally about 3 percent annually since 1955. Japan with its very high farm prices has had a larger annual decline in farm employment since 1955 than has Canada or the United States with their much lower prices (Johnson 1982). Nor have the higher EC prices prevented a more rapid rate of decline in farm employment than in North America. Of course, the rate of decline in farm employment would have been somewhat greater with lower farm prices than with those that prevailed. But differences in farm employment declines have been quite modest. High and stable farm output prices encourage increased capital investment in agriculture, and thus substitution for labor. The high prices also encourage greater technological change and a probable reduction in the demand for farm labor for a given output level.

One consequence of the farm policies of the IMEs is very certain. The high prices bring forth increased farm production. They have brought forth unwanted production in Japan, the EC, and the United States in recent years. Both the United States and Japan have attempted to reduce the output effects of incentive prices and returns but such efforts have generally been relatively ineffective. In fact, we do not know for sure whether the combination of high returns and output limitations have actually reduced output in the United States from what it would have been with prices that were about the same as international market prices in recent years.

Food Security. In Japan the high farm prices—much higher than in the EC or the U.S. for grains and oilseeds—are politically supported because the high prices are said to contribute to food security. Food security is a legitimate concern. But the policies that Japan has been following do not contribute significantly to food security. Being self-sufficient in rice production while importing virtually all energy supplies does not provide nearly as much security as a well designed rice and grain storage program combined with a much lower level of rice production. I have concluded that the Japanese political parties, the Ministry of Agriculture, and farm groups have deliberately aroused and maintained the fears of the Japanese consumer concerning food security in order to obtain acquiescence in the high prices of rice and other food products.

Maintain Rural Communities. The third objective of the farm price and income support programs has been to maintain viable rural communities. There is no evidence that these programs have accomplished this. In the EC-10, less than 10 percent of total employment is currently in agriculture; in the United States the percentage is now less than 3. In Canada, only 5 percent of the labor force is now in agriculture compared to the 7 percent in Australia and 11 percent in New Zealand. What is abundantly clear is that viable rural communities now must have a significant non-farm source of employment other than servicing farms and farm people. Thus farm policy by itself cannot assure the maintenance of viable rural communities.

Stable Farm Income. To what degree have relatively stable nominal output prices achieved stability of farm incomes and asset prices? In the official pronouncements of the EC considerable emphasis is given to the desirability of achieving farm income stability, and it is often noted that value added per farm or per farm worker has been very stable. But stability of value added does not assure that the net income of farm operator families will be stable. Value added by agriculture includes not only the net returns to farm operator labor, management, capital, and land but also depreciation and interest paid. Table 4 presents annual percentage changes in the net incomes of farm operator families in the United States and in four EC member countries. Even the most casual inspection of the data reveals enormous year-to-year income instability. Much of the instability arose from the effects of macroeconomic policy, especially through interest rate changes, and not from output price changes. Not only are high output prices ineffective in assuring farm people that they will share in economic growth, but stable output prices are insufficient to assure stable incomes.

Table 5 presents data on annual percentage changes in real prices for total farm land in the United States, two regions in the United States, and five EC members. Large annual variation in farm land prices in the United States is something that we all know about. Rather less well known is that the CAP has not prevented wide swings in land prices in the EC.

But even if policymakers can intellectually accept the ineffectiveness of the price and income programs that they have supported for decades, they still face the extremely difficult and practical problem of extricating themselves and farmers from the mess they have created. Though incomes are not significantly increased by continuation of the existing programs, abandoning or greatly limiting the price interventions and subsidies will cause considerable hardship and economic adjustments. Farm families—millions of them—have made commitments of time and resources based on the continuation of existing programs. Many of them have incurred debts, backed up by asset values based upon the current programs. The programs have encouraged the creation of excess production capacity, and as incentives are reduced, resources must be withdrawn from agriculture. This is a difficult undertaking unless it occurs

Table 4
Year-to-Year Changes in Real Net Farm Operator Income: United States, Denmark, France, Germany, and the United Kingdom, 1974 to 1985[a]
(Percent)

Year[b]	United States	Denmark	France	Germany	United Kingdom
1974	−27	−16	−15	−18	−24
1975	−15	−41	−13	20	0
1976	−26	−6	−1	5	11
1977	−8	22	−2	−5	−12
1978	18	−1	1	−6	−11
1979	0	−78	0	−17	−22
1980	−47	−89	−19	−22	6
1981	52	754	−4	8	12
1982	−21	196	28	30	6
1983	−45	−46	−13	−34	10
1984	142	161	2	32	−7
1985	−10	−4	−15	−22	−4

Source: U.S. Department of Agriculture, Economic Research Service, *Economic Indicators of the Farm Sector: National Financial Summary, 1985*, ECIFS 5-2, pp. 14 and 24, and European Community, *Agricultural Incomes in the European Community in 1985 and Since 1973*; European Community, *NEWSFLASH*, Green Europe, April 1986.

[a]Net income of farm operator families from farming due to production for the calendar year with net incomes in current national prices deflated by gross national or domestic product price deflators.

[b]The year indicated is the second year of a comparison—e.g., 1974 row compares the change in real incomes in 1974 to the 1973 incomes. The percentage change is calculated as the ratio of one year's income to the prior year's income minus one and multiplied by 100 to transform into percentages.

over a lengthy period of time. Even then there will be many who will suffer substantial asset losses.

Many families would have sought alternative livelihoods at an early time in their working lives when change would have been much easier and less risky. Many may feel embittered because their government has misled them with respect to the long-term prospects for profitable employment in farming. Consequently the politicians have to accept some risk in "telling it like it is," namely that the current programs were not only costly to consumers and taxpayers but were ineffective in providing higher, more stable farm incomes and in creating a secure future for farm families. The politi-

Table 5
Annual Percentage Changes in Real Prices for Farm Land, 1971–1986[a]

	U.S.	Corn Belt	Northern Plains	U.K.[b]	France	Nether-lands	Denmark	Germany[c]
1971	−2	−4	−4	−12	–	–	−3	–
72	2	1	1	6	4	–	10	–
73	5	5	5	87	5	–	7	–
74	12	16	17	18	4	13	15	–
1975	2	4	10	−35	–	34	6	−3
76	6	15	10	−23	3	−8	8	5
77	9	23	7	7	2	40	3	14
78	2	2	−4	30	1	30	−11	11
79	8	5	7	8	5	−1	−5	14
1980	7	7	8	10	−12	−13	−14	13
81	1	−1	1	−12	−9	−28	−25	5
82	−6	−14	−4	–	−11	−17	−21	−10
83	−8	−17	−7	4	−10	12	−5	−1
84	−5	−8	−9	–	–	–	–	–
1985	−16	−27	−24	–	–	–	–	–
86	−15	−17	−18	–	–	–	–	–

Source: U.S. Department of Agriculture, Economic Research Service, *Agricultural Outlook*, June 1986 and *Agricultural Statistics, 1980*, and Commission of the European Communities, *The Agricultural Situation in the Community*, various reports.

[a]Prices in national currencies deflated by gross domestic product implicit price deflator.
[b]England and Wales from 1971–1977; England from 1978.
[c]Data prior to 1974 not comparable to 1975 and later.

cians must now face the voters they have cultivated for many years and take the risk that they will lose voters' support in the future.

Improving Market Access for Developing Countries

Over the next few years the best approach for improving market access for the developing countries is through GATT negotiations that reduce the protection afforded agriculture in the industrial market economies, as well as in the higher income developing countries.

In a recent article, Alberto Valdes (1987) summarized studies that he and Zeitz had undertaken to project the effects of trade liberalization by OECD countries upon the exports of agricultural products by developing countries. One study indicated that a 50 percent reduction in protection levels that existed between 1975 and

1978 would have increased LDC exports of agricultural products by about 11 percent or nearly $6 billion (1985 dollars). OECD protection levels were significantly lower between 1975 and 1978 than between 1979 and 1981, and lower between 1979 and 1981 than since then. Estimates were made (Valdes and Zeitz 1986) of the LDC increase in exports for four farm products—sugar, beef, wheat, and maize—that would have resulted from full liberalization of the 1979-81 protection levels. Depending on the assumptions made concerning elasticities of supply and demand, the increase in the value of exports (1980 dollars) ranged from a low of $8.35 billion to a high of $12.4 billion. Protection levels for sugar were much higher in 1983 (and since) than between 1979 and 1981. Liberalization of world sugar trade in 1983 would have more than doubled the export gains projected for the period of 1979 through 1981.

The EC has been a net exporter of sugar for several years as a result of domestic producer prices that have been two to four times world market prices for most years since 1970. The United States is well on its way to completely eliminating sugar imports; in the early 1980s we imported approximately four million metric tons of raw sugar. During 1987, our imports of raw sugar were less than one million metric tons (USDA September 1987, 18). In 1986, the United States followed EC practice and heavily subsidized the sale of some 150,000 metric tons of sugar to China; the price was $105 per ton compared to a cost to the U.S. government of at least $450 per ton. The subsidy to accomplish the sale, made in competition with developing country producers and with one of our staunchest allies (Australia), was about 3.5 times the price realized (USDA September 1986, 14).

Occasionally, the public relations arm of the U.S. government attempts to put a favorable gloss on the effects of the Caribbean Basin Initiative. What modest positive benefits may have occurred have been far more than offset by the loss of access to the U.S. sugar market. The decline in U.S. sugar imports has resulted from high producer prices for sugar that have encouraged increased domestic production of cane and beet sugar (about a quarter since

1980) and has created a market for high-fructose sugar made from corn. This high-fructose corn sweetener (HFCS) has increased its share of the caloric sweetener market in the United States from 12 percent in 1979 to 35 percent in 1987. The increase in HFCS consumption was 3.6 million metric tons, approximately equal to the decline in imports of raw sugar (USDA September 1987, 360).

Consumption of all forms of corn sweeteners now exceeds the consumption of sugar in the United States. The domestic political pressures for continuation of protectionist policies for sugar are now stronger than ever. The small number of sugar farmers (fewer than 12,000), sugar refiners (fewer than 50), and processors of HFCS (fewer than 10) are now joined by several hundred thousand corn producers who are now enjoying the benefits of a highly subsidized demand for their product. About one-tenth of the domestic demand for corn is for sweeteners, and alcohol accounts for an additional 5 or 6 percent of domestic use (USDA November 1987, 14).

Alternatives to General Trade Liberalization

What alternatives to trade liberalization have been proposed to A.I.D. developing countries in their trading with the IMEs? Two alternatives that have been proposed are commodity agreements and revisions and extensions of the generalized system of preferences to effectively include most, if not all, agricultural products. Neither alternative has ever transferred significant benefits to most of the developing countries.

Commodity Agreements. The history of commodity agreements for agricultural products has been, to put it mildly, a checkered one. Currently there are four such agreements in effect—cocoa, coffee, rubber, and sugar. None has been effective in minimizing price variability, generally the avowed objective of the agreements (World Bank 1986, 136). Commodity agreements are not a means to increase trade in agricultural products. Generally such agreements are designed to restrict trade in order to raise and stabilize prices. If the agreements fail to restrict trade, either due to cheating by the signatories to the agreement, or by expanded production and exports by countries who are not participants in the agreement, they are considered to have failed.

Commodity agreements, if they are to benefit the producer members, must do so by increasing prices, which, of course, has results quite opposite to that of expanding trade. Thus in no sense are commodity agreements trade liberalizing measures. And there is no support from history that agricultural commodity agreements can be used to increase export prices enough to increase export revenue for any significant period of time. We know all too well from our own domestic experience that price-increasing measures result in excess capacity and excess supplies and that the higher prices are sustainable only by resort to government subsidization. Because of the conflicting interests of exporters with respect to sharing of costs for enforcement of commodity agreements, the agreements are soon ineffective due to a failure to restrain production or to increase stocks sufficiently to hold prices within the agreed price range. It is trite to say, but nonetheless true, that if international market prices are to be increased, exports must be reduced below the amount that would otherwise be forthcoming. Thus liberal or free trade and commodity agreements are not synonymous—quite the contrary.

Generalized System of Preferences. I have said for more than two decades that trade preferences given by the industrial countries for developing country imports are a fraud. They are, however, a fraud perpetrated as much by the so-called leaders of the developing countries as by the countries that engage in such false generosity. The Generalized System of Preferences (GSP) has been a failure, both generally and for agricultural products. One reason for this is that during the Tokyo Round negotiations, the existence of the system caused the representatives of UNCTAD to have an ambivalent attitude toward further reductions in tariffs. Any reduction in MFN tariffs reduced the advantage derived from a preference rate. Thus GSP helped to mute one of the voices that should have supported trade liberalization.

Why has GSP been a fraud? One only needs to look at what effect the schemes have had upon the exports of developing countries and especially of the lowest income countries. Approximately 2 percent of all OECD imports qualified for preferences, equivalent to 7 percent of developing countries' total exports (World Bank 1986, 142). Many, if not most, agricultural products are excluded. For example, the United States excludes sugar (because of the import quotas), dairy products, peanuts, and long-staple cotton from GSP and the Caribbean Basin Initiative as well. The United States excludes such products because increased imports would make it more difficult to maintain the price supports for domestic producers. The EC and Japan also exclude most agricultural products. Consequently, unless there is a radical change in the product coverages, GSP offers no significant prospect for increasing agricultural exports of the developing countries.

Some further general difficulties with GSP, as well as restricted preference schemes, such as the Lome Convention, may be noted. The preferences are almost never unrestricted; if imports of a preference item exceed a specified quantity, the regular MFN tariff applies. This seems both reasonable and simple. But it is not simple. If imports exceed the approved quantity, who decides who gets the advantage of the lower duty on the preference quantity? If the decision is left to the exporters, the decision will be made by some government office. If the decision is left to the importers, under some methods of allocating rights to the lower duties, most of the benefits will go to the importers with little left over for the exporters. Neither of these approaches, or any other with which I am familiar, contributes to a liberal trade regime. Instead, the GSP aids and abets governmental intervention in trade.

The GSP schemes generally will not be extended to most farm products where the levels of protection are high. Or if included, the effects are largely meaningless. The United States has included sugar in its GSP scheme. But the inclusion is largely meaningless. The inclusion permits duty-free entry but it has not protected the recipient countries from the near elimination of their share of the import quotas. And when other import quotas reach zero, there will be no benefit from the zero duty provision.

Conclusion

I shall conclude with a few comments concerning the GATT negotiations on agricultural trade with emphasis upon methods of measuring protection levels. There is general, though not unanimous, agreement among the OECD countries that Producer Subsidy Equivalent (PSE) is a useful tool to be used in the negotiations. It is useful in two senses: as a measure of existing levels of protection and as a monitoring device for evaluating progress toward liberalization. The PSE is a method of estimating the amount of transfers from the consumers and taxpayers to agriculture relative to the total value of agricultural output. The value of agricultural output includes, in addition to the free-trade or border price, both added costs imposed upon consumers through market prices in excess of border prices and any direct income payments to farmers. The transfers from consumers and the government are defined as policy transfers. The PSE is calculated as the percentage of total value of agricultural output due to policy transfers.

Earlier I have referred to levels of protection. These have been measures of nominal protection—generally the ratio of the domestic price to the border price (either import or export price as the case may be). In most cases the domestic price consists of the price received by farmers plus any direct payments made to the farmers, such as the deficiency payments in the United States. One source of confusion is that these seemingly similar measures of protection appear to give quite different results. The differences are due to several factors: the PSE includes a wider range of subsidies and income transfers than the nominal protection measures. The PSE includes some government costs that are not received by farmers, such as the cost of carrying large stocks of commodities under price support loans or the expenditures upon agricultural research and extension.

But the most important source of confusion is the choice of the denominators in the calculations. In the measures of nominal protection, the denominator is the value of the farm product at border prices—what the domestic price would be if there were free trade in that country. In the calculation of the PSEs, the denominator is the total value of agricultural output, including the income derived from policy transfers. The numerators may also differ somewhat—the PSE calculations include more subsidies and transfers than the estimates of nominal protection. There is no upper bound to the measure of the nominal protection; if the domestic price is five times the international market price, the nominal protection coefficient would be 4.0. (One is subtracted from the computed ratio so that when domestic price and border price are equal, the protection coefficient will be 0.) However, in the same situation, a domestic price five times the world price would result in a PSE of 0.80. If the world price is $200 per ton and the domestic price $1,000 per ton, the policy transfer would be $800 per ton. The nominal protection coefficient is ($1,000 divided by $200) minus 1; the PSE is the ratio of $800 to $1,000; the latter figure is the value of agricultural output in the domestic market. The theoretical upper limit of the value of a PSE is 1.00, while there is no such upper limit for the nominal protection coefficient.

The United States has made a major proposal at the GATT negotiations. This proposal includes the following: (1) a ten-year elimination of all agricultural subsidies that influence international trade, (2) a ten-year phaseout of all agricultural import barriers, and (3) a harmonization of health and sanitary regulations that affect agricultural trade. The U.S. proposal addressed the issue of what subsidies or policy transfers should be included. The proposal suggests excluding direct income or other payments to farm people that are decoupled from farm production and "true" domestic and foreign aid programs. The U.S. proposal does accept the inclusion of research and advisory (extension) services as a part of the PSE estimates of income transfers (USDA September 1987, 9-11).

While the U.S. proposal can be applauded for attempting to eliminate all barriers to trade in agricultural products, it embodies an objective that cannot be reached in a decade, if ever. Hopefully, our negotiators have in mind some level of protection that could be reached by the end of this century. And perhaps the level need not be the same for all countries. In terms of trade impacts, a PSE of 10 percent in the United States may have as great a relative impact on trade in agricultural products as one of 25 percent in Japan. This is nothing more than an illustrative comment. The relevant point is that the trade impacts of protection, compared to the free-trade situation, are a function of the elasticities of supply and demand for agricultural products in a country. The effects of the same levels of protection upon the volume and value of trade will differ significantly from country to country.

There is another and perhaps politically more important argument for agreeing to some relatively low average PSE for each country or area rather than a PSE of zero for all. In every OECD country there are certain "sacred cows." In fact, politically speaking, cows are among the sacredly anointed in North America and the EC, as well as in other countries in Western Europe, since dairy products are among the most heavily protected of the farm products. Thus, if the U.S. were to emerge from the negotiations with an agreement to achieve a PSE of 10 percent (a reduction of one-third from 1979–81 levels and by a little more than half the 1982–84 levels), it would be possible to provide moderate levels of protection for several of our sacred cows—dairy, sugar, peanuts, and wheat.[7] If there were agreement on what constituted income transfers that were decoupled from production, it would be possible to provide adequate transition or adjustment assistance for those agricultural sectors that would need to shrink more than average for all agriculture and to do so in a manner that minimized the pain and costs of adjustment.

Most of the means by which current agricultural policies transfer income to farm people are inefficient in the sense that the amount of net farm income generated represents only a fraction of the actual costs of the transfer. The major source of the inefficiencies in current methods of transfer is that the payments are either designed to induce farmers to produce more or are payments to farmers not to produce—to leave some of their resources idle. In either case there is a great deal of waste, and much of the transfers end up as payment for services supplied by persons who are not farmers or to compensate farmers for foregone opportunity.

If, instead of paying farmers to produce what we do not want or need, or paying them to leave some of their resources idle, we made no-strings-attached transfers directly to persons who are now farming, we could maintain the current level of farm family income at a much lower cost than what our farm programs now cost. After a period of years—perhaps a decade—we would have an agriculture able to compete in world markets without subsidies, with only limited and declining protected sectors. And gradually, if we had the political will, the total of the production-decoupled income transfers could be eliminated over time.

Comment   *Edward Schuh*

DR. SCHUH: Gale has given us an excellent paper. It seems to me that he has perceptively focused on the key issues and marshaled his arguments very, very well. One learns a great deal from the paper, and I would just say that it is too bad that we can't make it required reading for policymakers and trade negotiators alike.

There are a few points here and there in his paper that I might pick at a bit, but I prefer instead to use my time to broaden the agenda for the discussion. I want to broaden the agenda not only because I believe that Gale's paper is a bit narrow in the sense that it focuses almost exclusively on developed-country policies, but because the negotiations taking place in Geneva make the same mistake in my view.

I would like to address four topics: first, restrictions to trade by low-income developing countries; second, distortions in exchange rates as distortions to trade; third, intellectual capital in the case of agriculture; and fourth, adjustment policies.

So let me start with restrictions to trade by the developing countries. I am struck by the asymmetry in the agricultural negotiations that are currently underway, which doesn't make them any different than they have been in the past, but it still is rather striking in light of the additional knowledge that we have about some of these issues.

The negotiations focus almost exclusively on the problems of export subsidies, problems of access, and domestic policies which subsidize agriculture. By focusing on these issues, they direct us to the policies of the developed countries where such policies hold sway.

Unfortunately, the developing countries use trade restrictions as well. In most cases, however, these restrictions go the other way. They discriminate against agriculture by shifting the domestic terms of trade against that sector, not in favor of it.

There is a wide range of policies that are used to this end; probably the most widely used is overvaluing currencies, but on top of that, many countries have explicit export taxes. There are export quotas, there are complicated licensing procedures which restrict trade, et cetera.

I was struck when it used to be the case in Brazil, and I think this legislation is still on the books, that licenses for exporting agricultural commodities, particularly food commodities, were not granted as long as the domestic price was rising. Now you were doing that when domestic inflation was running 40, 50, 60 percent a year, so the decision rule almost inevitably gave you the result that you couldn't grant the export license. The whole purpose of that, of course, was to keep domestic food prices low for urban consumer groups.

My point is that these policies by the developing countries are every bit as important in distorting global resource efficiency in agriculture as are the policies and programs implemented by the developed countries.

In fact, I would say that, empirically, these policies may be more important in distorting global resources than are the policies of the developed countries. I say that based both on the size and prevalence of these kinds of distortions, and on the size and significance of agriculture in the developing world.

If the objective of the trade negotiations is to obtain a more efficient use of the world's agricultural resources by means of trade liberalization, then we should give the same attention to these distortions as we do to those by the developed countries.

The problem, I think, when you look at this is that you find that there is very little incentive to get these issues on the table. Certainly, the United States and the EC are not going to be anxious to have these policy reforms because it is going to cause developing countries to increase their agricultural output, to become more competitive to increase their exports, et cetera.

Of course, the developing countries have little incentive to change these policies because they live by blaming all their problems on the policies of the developed countries. So they are not going to push these issues onto the table.

Let me just make two comments on this issue. Our notion is that changing these policies may be more growth-enhancing globally than changing policies in the developed countries; and as we think about the global scene, it is an important thing that we should keep before us.

The other point that I would make is that if we could get these kinds of reforms in the developing countries, I think we would put a lot more pressure on the developed countries to change their policies because it would make their policies much more expensive in terms of budget costs. Recognize that the developed countries are getting around their distortions by using export subsidies. The U.S. uses deficiency payments.

As more developing countries become more competitive, exporting more and driving world prices down, then the budget costs for the EC and the U.S. in particular, from their own policies would probably become very, very large.

One way that this wouldn't occur, of course, is if developed countries continued to implement supply management programs as Gale mentioned, but those programs have costs as well.

Let me turn to the second set of issues which is the distortion of exchange rates. This is related to my previous point, but it always surprises me how distortions of exchange rates seldom become an issue of trade negotiation.

They are treated almost completely as a monetary issue when, in fact, as we all know, distortions of exchange rates have their equivalence in trade distortions whether you are talking about an overvalued currency or an undervalued currency. They end up being tariff equivalents: implicit export subsidies, implicit export taxes, and what have you.

If we are going to broaden the agenda so that we look at both sides of this trade issue, then it seems to me that exchange rates and other distortions become terribly important. It is again the case, I suspect, that if one looks worldwide, particularly at the developing countries, that an overvalued currency is probably the most widely practiced trade distortion that these countries have.

One of the things that causes me to give this issue more attention is that I suspect that as we look to the decade ahead, the problem isn't going to be overvalued currencies, the problem is most likely going to be undervalued currencies; and that is equivalent to an implicit export subsidy. I think many of the debt countries are going to follow the road of Mexico and undervalue their currency as a way of earning foreign exchange.

There was an earlier period in our history when countries did a lot of that and it was a very pervasive "Beggar Thy Neighbor" policy. I really would argue very strongly that we get some rules and some discipline, if you will, against doing this.

There is another whole set of issues that has to do with the problem of monetary instability and the large swings in exchange rates that instability creates. These large swings then become the incentive for protectionist measures, and I think that we should be talking about that set of issues as well.

You may view it as getting us beyond the issue of the day, but I think it is still a very important issue. If we continue to take this narrow cut at our problem, we may end up missing some of the most important things that are going on out there.

The third topic that should be given more attention is the issue of intellectual capital for agriculture. There are two sets of issues here which I want to address briefly, but one of the main points that I want to make is to remind us of the significance of genetic material and biological improvement as a source of the progress in agriculture. Call it technological progress or what have you. Fundamentally, most of it comes down to the question of how to improve plant material and that sort of thing.

The thing that has happened on the world scene is that international research centers have set about trying to collect and assemble the germ plasm and plant material from a wide variety of sources. Part of this is just a pragmatic issue because they need as wide a variety of germ plasm as they can get to cross as a basis for improving the plant material.

But the other part of the issue is that there is a concern that as forests are cut down in the South American continent and in Africa, there is a lot of plant material being lost—and a concern that it is being lost forever; and that is a capital for the future of the world that we ought not just let disappear.

You get a response to these efforts to assemble germ plasm from developing countries that can only be described as emotional. They have the perspective that if you take a bag of seed out of the country, you have in a sense robbed that country of its virginity. They would have you believe that you have stolen something from them, and the implication is that by taking that sack out, there is absolutely nothing left back there. That is the nature of the discussion that one gets over these issues, and it has gone so far that many developing countries have actually passed laws now which prohibit the removal of plant material of any kind from their countries.

I can hardly imagine anything that is more counterproductive to their best interest, and it is the case that these laws cannot be very effective.

I happened to work at Purdue University when we helped the Brazilians improve their soybean varieties, and I consequently catch a lot of flack for my trouble. I always remind American farmers that the Brazilian farmers are not stupid and that they were traveling this country from one end to the other. There may have been laws against taking it out, but there are pockets, there are big overcoat pockets, and all kinds of ways that you can get that material out.

So eventually you can't put up a barrier to this kind of trade, but what you do is complicate the life of researchers and research institutions.

The other part of this issue is just the general failure in the negotiations to give much attention to protecting the rights of plant breeders—again, mostly in the developing countries.

The consequence of that, of course, has caused the private sector to underinvest in this kind of biological research in these countries. If they can't protect the investment that they make so that they can collect some of the economic rents, they simply don't do it. I think over the longer term, those kinds of laws, those kinds of protectionist measures, may be more important than the so-called prohibitions against taking out the material.

There is an intellectual capital item on the agenda in the political round. Most of it has to do not with this set of issues, which I consider to be fundamental to the interest of the developing countries, but with copyrights, not so much copyrights but pirating and copying and that sort of thing. Those issues are important to the industrial sector.

Let me now talk briefly about adjustment policies. I guess the question that I would raise here is whether we economists have been creative enough on this issue. I think the adjustment policy issue may be more important for agriculture than it is for manufacturing and other sectors of the economy.

There are two issues here. One is, as Gale has pointed out, the need to transfer resources out of agriculture as development proceeds. This is almost an inevitable characteristic of economic development, and you have to look long and hard to find any country where that hasn't been what has been required.

The second point, however, what makes that process difficult, is that out-migration from agriculture typically involves geographic migration. You are not just talking about changing employment in your same city or same town, but you are typically talking about pulling up your roots and moving from the south of a country to the north, or from the east to the west, or what have you.

I think there are two other issues here that we need to keep focusing on, and I think this is what gives the added importance to the adjustment policy issues. First off, the failure to make a rapid enough adjustment in labor from agriculture to the nonfarm sector is what often leads to protectionist measures.

This is a point that Gale discusses. The second point, which he also discusses, is that if trade is to be liberalized, the need for adjustment assistance becomes even more important because even in countries as developed as the United States, with such a small percentage of its labor force in agriculture, you are still talking about very sizable adjustment problems.

Adjustment problems are a lot easier to accommodate now than they were 20 years ago, but nevertheless they are serious. As I implied, the focus of the adjustment policies should be on labor adjustment.

That may sound obvious to many people, but if you look at what EC adjustment policies for agriculture have been, they have typically involved infusions of new capital, of additional capital, into the agricultural sector. This brings with it new technology so you get a significant increase in agricultural output as a consequence of it and actually very little adjustment.

The programs that we need to be talking about on adjustment policy range from formal schooling to training to information services for labor markets, that sort of thing.

Gale, in another paper of about a year ago, pointed out that there are three tendencies that governments around the world have vis-à-vis agriculture. One of them is to underinvest in agricultural research as indicated by the fact that the social rates of return to those investments are so high. Second, a general tendency to underinvest in the schooling for the rural population and in most countries that disparity is very large; it is still rather large even in the case of the United States today. And third, the general tendency is to underinvest in rural infrastructure.

My point is that adjustment policies don't have to be a drag on the economy. To the contrary, if you are talking about education and training, and if you are talking about strengthening the rural infrastructure, you are actually doing things that would promote development and growth and not things that would actually be constraints.

One of the advantages of strengthening the rural infrastructure, of course, is you get nonfarm economic activities locating themselves out in rural areas where the labor force is, and you facilitate this adjustment process.

If you talk about adjustment policies in the developing countries, what you have to deal with is the fact that food prices rise as a consequence of the kind of policies that I was talking about, so one needs to talk about targeted and feeding programs and that sort of thing.

Let me just conclude by saying that one of my major concerns with the whole set of negotiations that are going on now is that we really are taking on the agricultural side of it. We are taking a very narrow cut at the problem, and we may be missing some of the most important things that should be done and, in fact, could be done.

Discussion

DR. KRUEGER: We agree with all your points, I think, regarding restrictions in output from developing countries. However, I would like to leave the exchange rate distortion topic to this afternoon as we get to that part of the agenda dealing with institutional issues. It seems to me they would come in very heavily there but I think the intellectual capital, the adjustment policy stuff, is obviously important and it fits in with what Gale has done.

It seems to me that there are a number of issues up for discussion. The range is very broad.

DR. SCHUH: Excuse me, I don't want you to push off the distortions in the developing countries too easily. I think they are a terribly important set of issues.

DR. KRUEGER: Sure they are, but what we are talking about here, is what can our donor agencies do, i.e., U.S.A.I.D. and so on, in terms of the trade negotiations. We agree that there are other things, too. It is not that they are not important to that but where they come in there it seems to me is the issue.

I don't want us to spend much time today addressing developing countries' policies; our intent is to focus on what can be done with respect to the international agenda for expanding the opportunities for developing countries to be both contributory participants and beneficiaries of international trade.

In any event, Gale has raised a whole variety of issues to which you have added the intellectual capital and the adjustment policies issue, although Gale touched on that.

I hope the Cairns Group will come up again in the discussion because it is very important and suggests a number of pertinent questions which warrant discussion: to what extent does the Group in and of itself represent progress; to what extent does it represent a model for what other groups of similar interests might do; what are the centrifugal and centripetal forces within the Cairns Group; and are there ways in which the centripetal forces can be strengthened? In addition, a fair amount of attention should be accorded a very important insight in Gale's paper: that concerted policies for agricultural adjustment will make the whole thing much easier than policies individually undertaken; what kinds of mechanisms, what ways and means might enhance the prospects for this occurring? And finally, discussion should address the important point that very little has been done to convince policymakers that extant agricultural policies don't work; what can be done with respect to this?

It seems to me that in some sense we want to focus on what can be done given this diagnosis of the issues.

DR. WHALLEY: Gale's marvelous presentation demonstrates anew that the question is not whether liberalization of the international trading system should apply to agriculture, nor whether domestic agricultural policies should be liberalized, but, rather, how either or both of these changes can be effected. Unfortunately, I am perhaps less optimistic than Gale about the few positive forces for such change that were identified in his presentation.

One of the two principal reasons for my pessimism is that repeal of the British Corn Laws did not dampen the mercantilist spirit. Domestic agricultural policies that are more costly than beneficial to the entirety of their respective economies are perpetuated because some within those economies are receiving differential benefits from the policies, and those favored few fear being worse off in the event of liberalization. Typically, too, mercantilists' *perception* of the benefits they receive exaggerates their actual advantage. But whatever the gains, special interests exert intense effort to protect and reify their favored status by means of government agricultural policies. This effort has been successfully translated into the circumstances which Gale described.

Now, does it make sense to expect that these same forces for mercantilism—as against market forces induced by liberalization—will be any less adept at preventing international agreements which erode their positions than they have been domestically? I am inclined to think not. After all, each of the negotiators represents a government whose domestic policies have been influenced by these mercantile interests. Thus, we should expect GATT negotiations to parallel those within the governments that sponsor the negotiators. This means that each will have greater concern for what, and how much, each has to give up and/or might gain, than for determining how all, or even most, might be made better off. Incidentally, in terms of the theme of the series which includes this seminar, mercantile interests are opposed, by definition, to "including the excluded."

The other principal reason for my pessimism is that differences among members of the Cairns Group have already become evident. Though I agree with Gale that formation of this coalition is a positive sign, I suspect that this is more a commentary on how truly abysmal has been the past than of expectations for the future. And, though the Cairns Group has been very important in influencing the negotiating agenda in the run up to Punta del Este—in influencing what *might be* negotiated—it is unlikely to engender results that are much different from past agreements. Even if the Cairns Group was unified and able to unanimously agree to a single negotiator having full authority for committing each and all of its members, it would have to overcome the mercantile forces addressed by Gale's paper. In fact, however, those forces are already evident in accounting for differences emerging *within* the Cairns Group.

DR. MICHALOPOULOS: I am very glad to hear that there are some other people around the table who have some questions about the Cairns Group. Let me pick up on a point that Johnson mentioned and that is that in the past no more than two countries got together about anything in agriculture.

Of course, if several of the cereal producers get together, you have the possibility of them getting together in order to raise prices in agriculture through restrictions of supply. Developing countries, as a group, are net cereal importers. I could see a situation developing where the Cairns Group provides a forum for the exporters of cereals, whether they be developed countries or one or two of the developing countries, Argentina perhaps, to get together and make a deal on cereals which would result in a significant increase in the price of cereals. This may be detrimental to the developing countries as a whole because they are net importers of cereals.

The question then is, is it going to be possible for the Cairns Group, besides exerting pressure on matters pertaining to subsidies of exports by the developed countries and thus resulting in raising prices of cereal exports, to do something about other things which are of importance to the developing countries in agriculture? Specifically, is it possible to address commodities like beef and sugar which are the commodities where the developing countries are facing major problems of access?

Thus I support the perception that the Cairns Group was a useful concept to build pressure to bring agriculture into the negotiations, but what happens after that is far from clear at this point, and the Cairns Group contains some dangers for the developing countries in the agricultural area.

Let me make a second comment which is really related to Ed Schuh's point about the agricultural policies of the developing countries and whether they are brought into the negotiations. My own sense of this is that the negotiations are going to be complicated enough without having such issues included. I think it is probably best if the agricultural policies of the developing countries are addressed in other fora or with other vehicles, such as through the policy dialogue of A.I.D., or the World Bank.

DR. MARES: I had a couple comments about this last point and that of Ed Schuh. Whether we explicitly address LDC agricultural policies or not, they are going to be part of the agenda because they are going to be impacting upon developed countries negotiators as they think about what it is that they can do about opening up their markets, and what impact that is going to have on international agricultural trade.

But I think that the last comment is really important. There are other fora that exist for influencing *developing* country agricultural policies. We see it in the IMF, the World Bank, A.I.D., et cetera. But there are few fora for influencing *developed* country agricultural policies because they don't have to go to the IMF or the World Bank for structural loans, et cetera.

So really, these international trade negotiations are one of the few ways that we have for having an influence on developed country agricultural policy. I think that it is important to keep that distinction alive.

DR. MORSS: I want to make a macro point and a micro point. The macro point is that LDCs do better in an open, expanding global economy. Unfortunately, the developed nations have been able to coordinate their policies in a way to ensure the rate of economic growth needed to prevent both the developed and the developing countries from being afraid of excess capacity. When they are afraid of excess capacity, nations impose restrictions to protect their employment base. I suggest we postpone the trade negotiations for a year and see if we can get the Japanese, the Americans, and the Germans to move to increase global aggregate demand. The United States has just abandoned free trade in its overseas efforts and is working very hard to reduce its balance-of-payments deficit. This is likely to reduce global aggregate demand and increase the incentives for other countries of the world to follow restrictionist policies. The micro point I would make is that the place where I see either an A.I.D. or a World Bank official having the greatest impact on trade policy is deciding what price to use in costing out a project that is supposed to expand a country's exports in a certain area.

In light of what has been said here, I have great difficulty coming up with a defensible way to assign prices. Benefit-cost analyses used to determine the viability of investments are insufficient. My guess is that if we went around the room and took a concrete project and asked everyone to assign a price to it, we would have a tremendous variance in terms of the prices we all assigned to it.

The point is that world prices of almost all commodities are rigged, depending largely on policies followed by Western nations. I think the tables in Dr. Johnson's paper make just that point.

That gets you back to a very fundamental operational question and that is, what sort of price do we assign in investment analyses, and I think that is where the A.I.D. officials at the working level and the World Bank officials have the greatest opportunity to influence trade policy.

DR. ORDEN: I would like to interject a couple of questions into our discussion. The first one is: Professor Johnson cites excess capacity as one of the major barriers to achieving trade liberalization; whereas it seems a lot of the discussion of the possibility of progress in the agricultural trade negotiations in the Uruguay Round is based on the enormous cost in the various countries of, in fact, supporting that excess capacity.

So I would like to have you discuss the distinction between excess capacity and excessive cost a little bit, and comment on whether you think we are at a unique point in terms of, at least, the major players' view of trade liberalization because of the costs they are incurring.

Second, there seems to be a common basis already afloat around the room that agricultural trade negotiations are going to go better if we all jump in the pool together. There has been some question already raised about that, about whether the agricultural trade negotiations will actually be a point at which instead of jumping in the pool and liberalizing, we jump in the pool and form one of Andy Schmitz's cartels.

The point has been raised by Robert Paarlberg in a recent paper and probably in the one Professor Johnson cites as well.

He considers, for example, one of the major problems in agri cultural trade to be the EC in the sense that by agreeing to a common policy, they raise their level of protection to that demanded by the most protectionist of the countries, which he cites as Germany. He argues that we might have, in reality, more trade in agriculture, if countries like France, for example, had the lower levels of protection that they might have naturally if they were not part of the EC.

So this is an example of where the negotiations may take us astray instead of taking us towards progress. If that is a possibility, just a possibility, it raises two questions. One, what are the probabilities in the real world that we are going to get more trade liberalization in agriculture by negotiations versus not having negotiations? This question is one that maybe is too political, Anne, given your earlier comments.

But the second, and I think a really important question, is what are the economic implications of liberalizing by yourself. It seems to me that A.I.D. and the World Bank and others are pressuring individual small countries to liberalize, and there is a great conflict between what the U.S. is doing and what the U.S. is saying others should do at this point.

So I think we ought to give some thought to what will happen if negotiations break down or don't make any progress, just sort of putter along. What pressures can be brought to bear, and what would be the economic consequences if some of the major players, as well as some of the smaller countries, actually liberalize their agriculture? Of course, this raises another issue. It is that I am not sure that, as a profession, we should put all of our eggs in the basket of arguing that all countries jumping into the pool together is going to lead to the solution to agricultural trade distortions.

If we do, and it fails, I think our credibility will be further damaged in terms of pushing for liberalization either in the U.S., the EC, or in the developing countries.

MR. GALLAGHER: I think Professor Johnson's paper does a good job on the first line of the title, but I think Professor Schuh did have very good questions about what impact this may have on the developing countries. Since we are not to talk about policies within those developing countries, and we are not to talk about over-valued exchange rates, it makes my question a little more difficult.

Nonetheless, it is not clear to me what the interests of the developing countries are in these trade negotiations. If we forget about whether or not they participate in these trade negotiations, fine, but what is their interest in these trade negotiations?

From the tables here it looks that if we have a liberalization of trade in agricultural products in general, this should bring world prices down. It seems to me that the existence of bad trade policies in most Third World countries, especially with regard to low prices for agricultural products, overvalued exchange rates, and nonfavorable terms of trade towards their own agricultural sectors, indicates to me that they should want prices to be down.

I am sorry, I made a mistake. The trade liberalization should bring prices up. And it doesn't seem that the Third World countries have the same interest from a consumer point of view as maybe we feel the developed countries do from a use of resources point of view. Am I wrong in this? Can somebody address this?

DR. JOHNSON: I will talk about it.

MS. SEIVER: I just have a comment on the Cairns Group. I don't think we should look at their role in the Uruguay Round too narrowly. By that I mean that I don't think their contribution goes as far as just getting agriculture on the agenda, because if you compare this Round with past Rounds, the Cairns Group, I think, has very effectively changed the whole atmosphere. This Round is not viewed as a North-South negotiation as far as the LDC's being sort of on the side.

I think they are really being brought into the GATT Round on a wider basis and beyond agriculture. An example, I think, is the United States considering where it can obtain support from some of the LDCs on the other issues in which it is interested such as IPR or trade-related investment.

Now they may not do much but the point is that the United States is considering that, and I think that is very significant compared to the last Round.

Another comment relates to how GATT negotiations really go in the give-and-take. I think we shouldn't forget that it is just not a matter of economics where when we give up something, the party on the other side will give up something or give something. It is really based on politics. For one thing, you can look at the speed of negotiations and what certain countries, or blocks of countries, will or will not do based on when their elections are scheduled. Also, just the political agenda and how they deal with the various political groups on an issue is important.

So I think that when we are talking about negotiating and give-and-take, you just have to remember that it is driven by politics as well.

DR. BALDWIN: I have a couple of comments. First, a general question, I wonder if someone could tell us just how the negotiations in agriculture are going in Geneva now, a little background. Are they just still putting proposals on the table? Is there any indication that there is the making of a compromise there? I would be interested in hearing about that.

A second matter is about trying to get a balance or reciprocity in these negotiations. I think in the past it has often been the thought that we would trade between the manufacturing sector and the agricultural sector.

In the last couple of negotiations, it was the idea that the Europeans would open up their agricultural markets and what they would get in return would be the opening of U.S. markets for manufactured goods.

But, in fact, what happened in these negotiations, and I would predict would happen again, is that it was very difficult to get a swap between the agricultural and manufacturing sectors and in the end, the manufacturing sector was not willing to make concessions in return for getting concessions in the agricultural sector.

There is just not a balance of political power between the two sectors that would make such an arrangement a viable option. We have seen, both in the Kennedy Round and the Tokyo Round, that agriculture gets sort of left out of the negotiations.

It would be nice to see a swap between the two sectors, but I am not too hopeful about getting a balance of concessions. So the question that Ed Schuh was talking about arises—namely, what kind of studies have been made about the possibility of getting rough reciprocity within the agricultural sector either by the LDCs opening up their markets in return for us opening our markets, or the developed countries opening their markets to each other.

Are there any sort of studies trying to get at this issue because as John says, "It is a fact of life" right or wrong, that unilateral liberalization is unlikely.

DR. KRUEGER: There is also a question within governments, because even if you could get those groups together, the fact that it is a ministry of agriculture there and a ministry of trade there is an institutional barrier of some magnitude.

MR. MASTERSON: In response to the last question regarding the status of the negotiations, the United States tabled its proposal on July 6, 1987, and proposals from other countries followed.

The Japanese completed the proposal tabling process in late December. The European Community, the Cairns Group, Canada, and the Nordics had advanced their policy recommendations in the intervening period.

At the December meeting of the negotiating group, the chief U.S. agriculture negotiator, Daniel Amstutz, suggested the need for more development on some of the key issues. To further this objective, the United States offered to present at the February session a discussion paper going into more detail on three major subjects: aggregate measures, harmonization of health and sanitary regulations, and decoupled payments. On another issue—that of special and differential treatment for developing countries—we endorsed the proposition of this being a legitimate area to be explored. Also, we volunteered to circulate a paper on S&D as soon as possible.

Decoupling of government payments from production and marketing decisions is so important—for it can correct the problem Gale Johnson has talked about today of the excess capacity and resources brought on by false incentive policies. Decoupled payments could be used in a transitional or safety net capacity as the world moved to a liberalized trading environment for agriculture. While academicians and agriculture economists have written much of late in praise of decoupled programs, less attention has been given to what definitions and rules might best apply. Is 100 percent decoupling feasible or to what degree of compliance should policymakers strive to attain?

Further work along these lines would be our proposed agenda for the GATT over the course of the next few months. Influencing the timing of substantive negotiations is the matter of the forthcoming French elections. Others have posited a delay may ensue because of the U.S. presidential elections. In response to the latter possibility, I would submit that the fact the U.S. proposal has bipartisan support and general agricultural industry endorsement should not be affected to any substantive degree by a change of administrations.

Technical progress can set the stage for consideration of a framework agreement on broad policy issued late in the year.

That is our plan. Driving the GATT negotiations in agriculture through the fast pace to date has, I believe, been the United States. Our far-reaching call for liberalized trade encompassing an end to trade-distorting subsidies, an elimination of access barriers and adoption of a harmonized system for animal and plant regulations has energized the debate.

Added to the dynamic force of our trade proposal has been the costly growth in export subsidy and general support programs. In particular, the Export Enhancement Program has helped to bring an earnestness to the multilateral process. It is only in the multilateral context, for that matter, that we see any realistic opportunity for correcting the distortions and disequilibriums which are so in evidence today.

Developing countries generally support our thrust of ending ruinous export subsidy practices, but sometimes they find little or no fault with their own protectionist policies. This dichotomy is certainly counter to trade liberalization, but I would submit is also contrary to long-term economic growth in the developing world. To gain more acceptance for liberalized trade, we dispel with clarity and precision one widely prevalent suspicion. That suspicion or doubt is that once all of the false incentives are removed, the resurgent economic benefits may not sufficiently fill the void. We are more convinced than ever of the economic vitality which will flow from a worldwide liberalized regime for agriculture. We encourage Dr. Gale Johnson and others to join us in making a convincing case for the growth which will flow from ending today's highly regulated and protectionist policies. Those are the major points I wanted to raise.

DR. CONYBEARE: I had three questions for Professor Johnson about the large adjustment costs in the developed countries. You suggested that the adjustment process should be slow, and it struck me that that is quite contrary to the deregulation literature in this country that says if you are going to deregulate, you should do it quickly.

When Alfred Kahn is asked why airline deregulation was so successful in this country he says, "Because we did it quickly." So I wonder whether or not slow is better than quick.

The second question is you say that the adjustment costs are very large and my response to that would be to say, "compared to what?" It is a small part of U.S. national income, and, I think, the human capital in agriculture is probably pretty mobile (the population of the state where I live has been dropping for five years). In so far as there are specialized resources in agriculture, they depreciate and I wonder how fast do they depreciate because once they are fully depreciated, there are no adjustment costs.

The third question is related to the literature on trade on the cross-sectional structure of tariff protection. Pincus, Caves, and others have done studies that look for the rent-seeking correlates of the cross-sectional structure of protection.

I was wondering if there has been work done like that in agriculture, because if it has, then that will give us some good clues as to where the major political obstacles are to reforming the agricultural sector in this country.

MR. SPOSATO: While I generally agree with the remarks and the presentations, I think it is appropriate to set Gale Johnson's paper in a larger historical context.

The problem of oversupply in agriculture is not a new phenomena. We have seen cycles of oversupply followed by cycles of shortages in agriculture consistently. One of the reasons for the large government intervention in agriculture is to prevent exoduses at the high points of oversupply and to prevent overentry at the low points, to prevent all the social chaos and market chaos that this causes.

Even if we go back to the high prices in the 1970s, which were probably caused largely by natural causes, we see in the late 1960s destocking of U.S. stocks. So while there do seem to be fundamental productive differences today that may lead us to believe that the oversupply is more durable and here to stay, there are other indications. The very rapid change in the rice market is an indication of what can happen in agriculture.

I think there is a role for government intervention. It is not the role we have at present. I was very pleased to see you criticize the 1981 farm bill. I think you were criticizing the overhigh loan rates and target prices in that farm bill.

I think even more harmful under the 1981 farm bill was that the secretary did not use any of his authority for set asides, and this increased the cycle of overproduction until he entirely reversed policy with the PIK in 1983 or 1984.

So we do have a role in agriculture for government, and I think that we need to be aware of this role, aware of the problems that the European Community is concerned with and that Japan is concerned with which include food security and domestic production. These are still legitimate concerns. What we have to do is address the problems that can be addressed much better than in the manner that they are being addressed in those countries today.

DR. KRUEGER: Ten years ago our policy was discussing food shortages. Now, of course, you have a national policy that has led in the opposite direction. One kind of idle thought might be that, yes, right now might not be the ideal time to restructure, but might it not be the time to start thinking (if indeed it is not already too late) about policies that could be put in place so that as the next response to all these government policies appears and people begin going to higher prices, one could at that time phase out in some reasonably sensible way?

Response

D. Gale Johnson

DR. JOHNSON: I think we can say about agriculture, at any given time, that things are never as good as they seem, which was true of the 1970s, and they are never as bad as they seem, which was true of the situation around 1985. We are always going up and down and around.

I think we are now moving out of the worst point of the situation in the mid-1980s, and international market prices are strengthening. The sharp rise in metal prices and industrial products are probably a precursor of significant increases that are going to follow in agricultural commodities.

However, I think comment about the 1970s went too far. I don't agree that the increase in prices in the 1970s was primarily related to agriculture. The subsequent evidence does not indicate significant shortfalls in the world production of anything. In 1972 and 1973 and 1974 some of the intelligence quotes at that time implied there were small fallouts.

But I think the price increases were primarily a consequence of macro policies, principally the response of industrial countries to the first oil shock and, in fact, these high prices were of remarkably short duration. They brought about their downfall very quickly. They essentially disappeared by 1975 and then strengthened later.

A number of you have raised the question of whether the negotiations are worth doing. Should we liberalize by ourselves—do it alone rather than jointly on the grounds that economists have argued that it pays to liberalize?

I don't think this takes into account essentially the power (political power) that farm groups have in all of the industrial countries and that is also related to the question on adjustment costs, whether you should go about it slowly or rapidly, that is, should you cut off your tail an inch at a time or take a whole whack at it. That is the basic issue.

We have at least one example in the United States that we were able to liberalize our domestic farm policies and do it slowly and this was the period from the mid-1950s to 1970. We went through a significant adjustment of agriculture which resulted in the essential elimination of excess productive resources by 1970, if we take into account the overvaluation of our currency at that time.

This could not have been done all at once. In fact, John F. Kennedy tried to force agriculture into a cold bath in 1961 and got beaten, and he had to continue the gradual policies that were started under the Eisenhower administration and by some means we were able, through four administrations, to maintain a given policy in this country. It is almost a miracle that we could do that. In most other areas, we have never carried out any one thing for that long.

In a talk I gave in Geneva, I did make a point somewhat similar to one that was made here about countries getting together and ending up making a deal on cereal. I have less concern about that than I have with the EC and North America getting together on a deal on supply management.

If you want to worry about anything, worry about that one as being the kind of deal that we are willing to accept with the EC to get any kind of a completion of trade negotiations. We are going to give a great deal of weight to supply management in the calculation of the PSEs, the producer subsidy equivalent.

In fact, this idea is included in the EC document they put on the table in Geneva, but the Canadians, what happened to you? You said that you should give credit for supply management, too. Supply management should not get credit for reducing current supplies in the estimations of the degree of protection or their trade impact. Supply management does not provide for long-run liberalization. That is what I think we should worry about rather than a cereals agreement. We haven't been able to make one of those stick internationally yet, but agreeing on supply management as meeting a large part of our trade liberalization obligation is a real concern to me.

There were a couple of comments related to whether excess capacity was a problem or the high cost of farm programs. I have ridden the high-cost roller coaster for some years hoping that it would be what would bring some sanity to farm programs. It hasn't brought it, and I don't think it is going to.

Legislatures don't really care about the consumer in most cases when it comes down to farm policy, it is only what the exchequer has to put up with that they really give much weight to.

It is certainly true in Japan, it is certainly true in the EC. The Commission in the EC hardly ever talks about consumer prices in its annual reports on agriculture in the Community. Certainly, the Japanese make nothing of it at the ministry level. That is the way it is.

In fact, as far as the United States is concerned, things are getting better. The costs of the farm program are going down, not because of anything that Congress did but because of small improvements in the international market prices.

Our farm programs are costing about two or two and a half percent of federal expenditures, and that is where they were in the 1960s—that seems to be tolerable.

A related comment was on what are the adjustment costs in agriculture; this gets back to the issue someone raised about land prices. A good part of the related costs if you have rapid adjustment in agriculture are what is going to happen to land prices.

I would say that in the United States if we took a cold bath on farm programs that land prices would fall somewhere between $50 and $100 billion dollars. This is after their having fallen half already, and I am not sure that the local institutions related to agriculture could stand up much further.

DR. KRUEGER: What percentage is that?

DR. JOHNSON: It is about 10 to somewhat less than 20 percent. Total land values are now about $550 billion. The potential loss in land values is a significant number, but it is not altogether its size but simply the fact that it is already on top of a decline that has put a great deal of pressure on credit institutions and other institutions serving agriculture.

Now if you think we can stand that then you should get out there and vote for it, but I think that we have to go about it more gradually than that. In the case of Japan, I did something a few years ago for publication, and then whomever I did it for did not want to publish it so I haven't carried it out, which was comparing changes in agricultural land prices in Japan starting in 1929 with what had happened in the American Midwest up to 1981.

I was flabbergasted to learn, and there may be good reasons for this, that the increase in Japan's land prices was no more than it was in Iowa. In other words, the high prices of rice and so on in Japan are no more effective in increasing land prices than the U.S. farm programs with their much lower prices.

Now there are many reasons for that, one of which is, it ain't so, that the price index for Japan from 1939 to 1950 ain't worth a damn! That is one possibility.

[Laughter.]

Because it went up something like 20-, 30- or 40-fold, and there may be an error there, but the other is that the Japanese land policy has attempted to maximize the cost of Japanese agricultural products, the cost of producing them, I would say. That has been its consequence.

The fact is that farm size hasn't increased to anything like it has in Western Europe with the very dense populations and so the costs in Japan are high particularly for producing rice and other products. So I don't know.

In Japan if you revitalize its agriculture by reducing the restrictions that the government has put on agriculture, you might well not see much of the drop in land prices because the nonagricultural value of land in Japan is so great that this might not occur.

What are the interests of LDCs in trade negotiations? I think we have overemphasized the possible effect of trade liberalization in increasing cereal prices and thus increasing some LDC import bills. A point that Alberto Valdes keeps making is that most of the discussions on the impact of trade liberalization on international market prices of agricultural products have dealt primarily with commodities of interest to the industrial countries except sugar. We don't look at the other commodities that are important in the export structure of the developing countries and if we take those into account—if we take into account their export-side potentials— then it is not obvious except for the countries that have mistakenly come to rely so heavily on cereal imports. As Ed Schuh says, they have held their own agriculture under restraint by overvalued currencies, export taxes, and low prices. It is such countries that would tend to lose because of the higher cereal prices.

This is an effect of trade liberalization that they would escape if they changed their own policies.

With respect to the Cairns Group, I know nothing about its internal functioning and whether they will be able to hang together. I certainly hope that they are able to hang together and are able to paper-over some of the important disagreements they have because, as I say, there needs to be someone out there to embarrass the rest of us, to do something.

Unfortunately, our skins are very thick in this area and it is going to take a lot of embarrassment and a lot of pressure to keep things moving, and I am pleased that the Cairns Group is there.

I will just make one final point and this goes back to what I started out with on oversupply. It is true that agriculture has been subject to cycles of abundance and higher prices and lower prices.

I don't think we can say that governmental intervention has done much to help prevent that. In fact, I would say right now the low state of international market prices in agriculture in the mid to late 1980s is a consequence of government policy. Had we taken the opportunity which we had in the 1970s to get rid of many of these agricultural policies, international market prices today would be significantly higher than they are.

Robert E. Baldwin

Increasing Access to Markets for Manufactured Goods: Opportunities in the Uruguay Round

Introduction

Conflicts between the developed countries (DCs) and less developed countries (LDCs)—due to their different objectives—arise in almost every subject being negotiated in the Uruguay Round. This paper will focus on the threat to less developed countries' market access in developed countries. This threat is posed by the breakdown of discipline in procedures regarding safeguard actions against injurious imports, countervailing duties responding to foreign subsidization, and duties to offset dumping. Specifically, procedural changes to improve market access for manufactures will be considered, together with possible rule changes relating to the LDCs that might make the DCs more willing to strengthen GATT rules on safeguards, countervailing actions, and antidumping measures.

Economic Growth, Industrial Adjustment, and Trade Policy

One of the most notable changes in the structure of world trade during the last 25 years has been the remarkable increase in developing countries' exports of manufactured goods to the industrial countries. The share of total imports of manufactured goods going to the developed countries from the less developed countries rose from 6.5 percent in 1963 to 14.5 percent in 1984.[1] The United States has been a major recipient of these goods, especially in recent years. Between 1977 and 1984, the U.S. market absorbed 63 percent of the $78 billion increase in LDC exports of manufactures to the DCs, raising its share of LDC manufacturing exports to the DCs from 40.1 percent in 1977 to 55.1 in 1984. The distribution of these exports among the developing countries has been highly concentrated. Seven countries—Taiwan, South Korea, Hong Kong, Brazil, Mexico, China, and Singapore—supplied 70 percent of the total exports of the LDCs to the DCs.[2]

The effect of this increase in exports of manufactured goods on growth rates in the LDCs has been unmistakable; those whose exports have shown the most growth have been among those with the most rapidly growing economies. The importance of export expansion as a powerful engine of growth has been recognized since Adam Smith's analysis of the development process, but recent advances in trade theory, involving dropping the assumption of constant returns to scale and perfect competition, have provided new insights into the understanding of export-led growth. One strand of the so-called new trade theory emphasizes the importance of start-up costs for firms, involving not only outlays on physical capital, but costs associated with developing a differentiated product that will gain consumer approval. As these firms expand, their average costs per unit of output tend to fall because of their ability to spread these fixed costs over a larger volume of output. Unit costs also tend to fall as employees' learning experience grows; as cumulated output rises, the proportion of output that meets acceptable quality standards increases.

These increasing returns imply the need for large markets for economic efficiency in many lines of manufactured goods. Access to international markets is one way of fulfilling this necessary condition. Another way that would seem to satisfy this condition is the diversion of domestic demand for imported manufactured goods to domestic producers by means of high levels of protection. In general, the strategy of import substitution, which was followed by many developed countries in their early post–World War II industrialization efforts, has not proven effective in stimulating efficient production, perhaps mainly because when protection is introduced, competitive pressures on domestic firms are reduced. There are other reasons: 1) large markets permit firms to take advantage of scale economies, but firm managers must feel competitive pressure from foreign producers to actually fully exploit the advantage; 2) because there are many varieties of most manufactured goods, each requiring a large production volume to minimize unit costs, the domestic market of many countries is not large enough to reap the benefits of large-scale production; 3) being forced to purchase inputs from other inefficient domestic firms compounds the problem; and 4) the elaborate system of controls established to carry out import-substitution programs diverts the energies of entrepreneurs into rent-seeking activities. ("Rent-seeking" describes efforts to use political influence or anticompetitive practices to obtain a return higher than that available under competitive conditions.)

When a number of developing countries shifted from reliance on import substitution to a strategy giving more weight to export promotion, their success was immediate and dramatic. But soon they encountered another problem as they began, along with Japan and other industrial countries, to promote exports to older industrial regions such as the European Community and the United States. The adjustment problems caused by the increased import

competition led to successful lobbying in these regions for increased protection against Japanese and Third World exports. Thus,
starting in the late 1960s, the United States and the European
Community resorted to selective protection against Japanese and
LDC exports of manufactured goods in the form of voluntary export restraint agreements (VERs) and orderly marketing agreements (OMAs). The United States also withdrew many items from
its list of products to which the Generalized System of Preferences
(GSP) applies, especially those from the most successful of the
LDCs. In 1987 alone, zero-duty treatment on over $3 billion
worth of imports was withdrawn by the U.S. government.

In addition to the shift to a bilateral or unilateral approach to
deal with import competition, the United States and the European
Community have recently emphasized bilateral negotiations to
secure import liberalization in Japan and the developing countries.
President Reagan's recent announcement that trade sanctions
would be imposed against Brazil for its failure to grant access to
its market for U.S.-produced software illustrates this approach.
After bilateral discussions with the United States, South Korea
agreed last year to liberalize its imports of passenger cars, personal
computers, and electric generators, and to make large purchases of
U.S.-made machinery and aircraft. Taiwan has also recently liberalized imports of some sixty agricultural and industrial items in
response to U.S. pressure.

For the developing countries, there are important consequences
of this shift away from a multilateral approach in setting levels of
protection. It is no longer a question of whether special privileges
such as GSP treatment and exclusion from the reciprocity requirement will be withdrawn from the developing countries, but rather
of the conditions under which this withdrawal will occur and the
concessions LDCs will get for giving up these privileges. If the
LDCs sit on the sidelines in the Uruguay Round as they did in the
Tokyo Round, except to insist on special and differential treatment
in all negotiations, they are again not likely to gain much in the
way of increased access to the markets of the DCs. Moreover, the

LDCs will be drawn into bilateral negotiations one by one to face developed countries that have much greater bargaining strength, and, under such threats as reduced access to the DCs' markets, they may be pressured into opening their own markets without gaining much in return.

This opening may be helpful to them in the long run, but another negotiating approach is available which offers a higher probability of more meaningful concessions from the developed countries and an even better long-run outcome for all concerned: taking an active part in the Uruguay Round, exchanging trade concessions, and helping to formulate new GATT rules to limit the DCs' ability to impose discriminatory protection against the LDCs and to further open their markets. In return, the more successful developing countries would assume more GATT responsibilities, similar to those of developed-country members of the Agreement.

Market Access Issues

The major trading issues between the developing and developed countries are clear cut and well known. The LDCs' strongest demand is for not only continued, but increased, access to the markets of the DCs, especially on preferential terms. They have seen the highly beneficial results of export-led growth and know that open markets in the major industrial countries are vital to their continued development. The increase in protection in the developed countries in recent years is of special concern. While the developing countries want increased access to developed-country markets, many, in particular the less open ones, do not wish to face the displeasure of domestic producers in import-competing sectors by opening up their own markets.

Most developed countries are no longer willing to accept the argument that, because of the social need to raise the LDCs' very low income levels, the DCs should open unilaterally their markets to the LDCs' products. Leaders in the more advanced developed countries now generally believe that industrial imports from the

LDCs and from rapidly growing industrial countries such as Japan are having a significantly adverse effect on domestic employment and should no longer be permitted to enter on such unequal terms. They especially resent the LDC governments' promotion of exports through various subsidies while continuing to reserve important domestic markets largely for domestic producers. To correct this situation, they call for the gradual elimination of the special privileges GATT granted to the LDCs which permit these practices, and for these countries to open their markets much wider for both manufactured and agricultural goods.

Strengthening GATT Rules on Safeguard Action, Subsidies, and Dumping

Probably the most serious threat to the LDCs' market access goals is the weakening of GATT safeguard procedures. In recent years the DCs have not only introduced more import protection for manufactured goods but have increasingly resorted to country-selective protection through VERs and other means. Imports of automobiles, steel, footwear, and television sets have all been controlled in this manner within the last ten years.

A closely related development is the DCs' much greater use of countervailing and antidumping procedures to protect domestic industries. The number of countervailing and antidumping actions brought by developed countries increased from 124 in 1979 to 405 in 1982, with the proportion of such actions directed against developing countries rising from 17 percent in 1979 to 26 percent in 1982. Some argue that, because of their weaker test for injury and the selective nature of the protection they permit, these measures are being used inappropriately, when instead safeguard actions under Article XIX of the GATT should be used. If so, the developing countries must not only try to bring safeguard actions under greater GATT discipline, but also try to seek changes in the GATT codes covering countervailing and antidumping procedures.

Safeguards. In the Tokyo Round negotiations, the European Community's insistence that GATT safeguard procedures be changed to permit the selective application of protection precluded negotiation of a new safeguards code when the LDCs, the United States, and some other developed countries rejected the EC proposal. Community negotiators are likely to make this proposal again during the current negotiations. While the official U.S. position still supports the multilateral application of safeguard protection, there is also considerable support in the country for permitting selectivity—provided the concerned parties agree to it and other members are not damaged by trade diversion.

Citing the fact that many countries are now selectively applying import restraints and are unwilling to return to the use of the most-favored-nation (MFN) principle in cases of serious injury to domestic industries, some conclude that the rules must be changed to permit selectivity in these situations if the GATT is to play a central role in maintaining an open trading framework. The non-MFN treatment that already exists in GATT-sanctioned customs unions and free-trade arrangements and under the GSP is often cited as a reason that a shift to the selectivity principle should not be regarded as a significant change in the GATT.

The above argument leaves unanswered the question as to why countries abandoned nondiscriminatory protection in import injury cases in the first place. One reason frequently given is the necessity of providing compensatory cuts in protection of other products to the principal suppliers of the protected product, thereby reducing the risk of retaliatory increases in protection by these exporting countries. In negotiating VERs, only those few countries whose rapidly increasing exports are the major cause of the import injury are singled out, and even these countries do not receive compensation. There is also an underlying view that it is unfair to raise protection levels against countries whose exports have not increased enough to cause injury; it is also unfair for countries to increase their exports so rapidly as to cause serious injury in an importing country, especially if these countries are highly protective of their own internal markets.[3]

Those who favor keeping the unconditional MFN principle, and, in some cases, a tightening of its application, to curtail the spread of preferential arrangements, give the following reasons for their views. First, discrimination that will increase under selectivity will worsen international relations. Former Secretary of State Cordell Hull, one of the key persons in the establishing of the GATT, reasoned that "if we could get a freer flow of trade—freer in the sense of fewer discriminations and obstructions—so that one country would not be deadly jealous of another and the living standards of all countries might rise, thereby eliminating the economic dissatisfaction that breeds war, we might have a reasonable chance for lasting peace."

Second, conditional MFN and the bilateralism it produces result in a less efficient use of world resources; thus a reduction in world income and growth rates as low-cost producers are replaced by high-cost suppliers. Third, discrimination often fails to achieve its intended purposes due to shifts in supply sources; therefore, many workers in the injured industry remain unemployed, and firms operate at a low capacity level but do not seek other productive alternatives because they are led to believe that protection will remedy their injury. Finally, acceptance of conditional MFN in safeguard cases will open the way for the introduction of more trade restrictions, both directly and through retaliatory actions, and will further undermine the GATT. The changing patterns of comparative advantage and the nature of economic and political power in the world economy make it likely that the developing countries will bear the brunt of these new restrictions.

There clearly must be a large judgmental component in viewing the relative merits of conditional versus unconditional MFN. If the international trading order continues to deteriorate due to the demise of the unconditional MFN principle, and if the trading world is so imperfect regarding competition that an active, aggressive trade policy is needed to prevent exploitation, the case for conditional MFN has merit. Unfortunately, we do not have enough historical experience to judge the first point nor enough empirical evidence on the second to reach a firm conclusion on this interpretation of the nature of the international trading regime. But the potential political and economic costs appear to be so large, and the uncertainty about the policy's effectiveness is so great, that it seems prudent to explore less radical changes in GATT rules before abandoning this cornerstone principle of the organization.

Eliminating the compensation requirement, provided the MFN protection was time-limited and degressive, would meet one of the most frequently heard objections to the present GATT rule. If the increased protection continued beyond a certain period of time—say, five or ten years—exporting countries would be free to demand compensation or else retaliate. Foreign suppliers whose exports to the protecting country have not increased significantly will obviously exert pressure on the country not to protect. This pressure will become a desirable feature of safeguard provisions. Import-injured industries in most countries usually succeed in forcing their governments to impose protection, though the long-run interests of the country are best served by allowing resources to be shifted to alternative economic activities. Pressure from foreign governments can serve to offset these pressures from industries. Thus the developing countries should continue to resist selectivity in safeguard actions but support the elimination of the compensation requirement under carefully specified conditions. The economic interests of the United States are also best served by opposing the selectivity principle.

If members agree to reject the selectivity principle, existing VERs and other selective measures should be gradually eliminated. They should be phased out entirely within three to five years or transformed into protective measures that are consistent with the MFN principle.

Subsidies and Countervailing Actions. For many years the United States has been the principal proponent of a tightening of the international rules on public subsidies and, as noted earlier, has frequently imposed countervailing duties against foreign products which are subsidized. At U.S. insistence, a subsidies code was negotiated during the Tokyo Round, but it is too ambiguous to be very effective. Countries that continue to subsidize justify their actions under this statement in the code:

> Signatories recognize that subsidies other than export subsidies are widely used as important instruments for the promotion of social and economic policy objectives and do not intend to restrict the right of signatories to use such subsidies to achieve these and other important policy objectives which they consider desirable . . .

In contrast, U.S. officials point out that the signatories have also agreed to seek to avoid using subsidies that "may cause or threaten to cause injury to a domestic industry of another signatory or serious prejudice to the interests of another signatory or may nullify or impair benefits accruing to another signatory under the General Agreement." The choice of this emphasis reflects the widely held view by U.S. producers that foreign subsidies have, in fact, caused material injury to many domestic producers and that the increased use of countervailing duties is justified as a means of trying to restore a "level playing field."

Because of the general acknowledgement that the subsidies code has been ineffective in this area, the ministers who met to inaugurate the Uruguay Round established a separate negotiating group on subsidies to improve GATT disciplines in this area. By the fall of 1987, three sets of meetings had been held. The group disagreed on whether to focus first on basic definitions and concepts or to concentrate on how to deal with trade-distorting subsidies. Those favoring the former approach wanted agreement on the definition of a subsidy and how it should be measured; others believed this might delay the work of the group and pointed out that existing disciplines have been developed without the benefit of agreed definitions.

The same basic issues will arise no matter which route is followed. The question is not so much what a subsidy is, but what types of subsidies should be "actionable," that is, subject to countervailing duties. Economists would say that production is being subsidized when the government provides assistance to a firm at a cost below that available in the private marketplace. But most would also say that not all subsidies should be countervailed. Some subsidies offset existing market distortions and tend to make the competitive playing field more level rather than tilting it. Looking at the matter from the viewpoint of those who wish to discuss how to deal with trade-distorting subsidies, not all subsidies distort trade from what it would be in a world without domestic distortions. Trade economists have long stressed the appropriateness of subsidies when imperfect capital and labor markets exist or when external economies are present in an industry. The recent integration of various concepts from industrial organization theory into trade theory suggests that subsidies can sometimes be welfare-increasing for a country if the industry receiving the subsidy competes internationally in imperfect markets or if there are dynamic scale economies associated with investment in knowledge in an industry.

There may also be a role for subsidies as an adjustment measure. Industries with net export balances sometimes suddenly lose markets to foreign competitors just as import-competing industries do. In these situations, import protection is not effective in easing the adjustment problems of the industry's workers and capital owners, whereas a temporary domestic subsidy can accomplish this goal.

A more explicit recognition in the subsidies code of the legitimacy of subsidies in some circumstances, and an elaboration of these circumstances, seems necessary for reducing the range of disagreements in this field. But provisions are also needed to prevent domestic subsidies from going beyond their purpose of just offsetting some domestic distortion, at limiting their duration, and at ensuring that they are degressive. Requiring full and regular reporting on the magnitude of government assistance and the extent to which it is achieving its purpose and improving on the dispute settlement mechanism in this field is an essential element of a revised subsidies code. Trading partners with countries whose assistance to domestic industries is consistent with these rules would not impose countervailing duties during the temporary period of the subsidies.

Another approach that complements efforts to introduce more substance and detail into the subsidies code is negotiating recipro-cal reductions in subsidies in a manner similar to the item-by-item, tariff-cutting technique used in the early days of the GATT. This approach could prove useful in dealing with long-established subsi-dies that are politically difficult to eliminate unless some meaningful trade concession is obtained from other countries. The objective would be to phase out particular subsidies gradually, bind subsidy levels for specified periods of time, or perhaps introduce export taxes (where permitted) to offset the export-subsidizing element in domestic subsidies.

Dumping and Antidumping Duties. According to the anti-dumping code negotiated in the Tokyo Round, dumping occurs if a product is sold in a foreign country at less than its normal value. More specifically, dumping takes place if the price the exporting country charges one country is less than the price it charges domes-tically or to other countries. In the absence of information on these prices, the normal price can be taken to be the cost of production in the country of origin plus a reasonable amount for administrative and selling costs and for profits. When dumping is established and it is determined that a domestic industry is materially injured, the code permits the imposition of an antidumping duty against the offending country equal to the dumping margin.

The initial purpose of antidumping laws was to prevent foreign firms from driving domestic firms out of business by using the profits they earned on high-priced sales in their own home market to keep domestic prices at below unit costs. The fear was that these compa-nies, after driving competing local firms from the scene, would raise prices to high levels. The intent of antidumping laws seems to have gone beyond stopping predatory dumping, however. The use of profits at home for what is considered, in effect, the subsidization of export sales is regarded as an unfair trade action. One might think the reasons foreign firms could charge a higher price at home, e.g., whether their governments were protecting their home markets by imposing trade barriers or whether normal differences in transportation costs were the reason, would play a role in an assessment of "fairness," but this does not seem to be the case.

A problem in trying to prevent dumping is that selling in different markets at different prices is a business practice that arises from normal competitive pressures. For a profit-maximizing firm, the market for a product in one country is differentiated from a market for the same product in another country in much the same way as the markets for two similar, but not identical, products sold within one single country. The firm will set profit-maximizing prices in each market, subject to the constraint that the price differential between the products or markets cannot be so large as to permit the product in one market to capture the other market by being shipped into that market. Whether overhead charges are being met from sales of another product or the same product in another market is of little concern to the firm.

The pressures to set different prices in different markets are especially strong for new export-oriented firms, such as those in developing countries that are starting out with only a few product lines. Since learning by doing is an important factor in achieving lower unit costs in most manufacturing activity, new firms competing against established producers in foreign markets are forced to sell below unit costs until they gain production experience, even if they begin with an optimum capital stock. These firms may even have to sell below the prices of the established producers in order to overcome buyers' reluctance to switch to allegedly comparable products. They usually do not have the kind of facilities to compete on the basis of customer services that established firms have. Charging higher prices in their home markets may be their only means of reducing losses to acceptable levels.

New firms are especially disadvantaged when administering authorities construct the normal value from cost-of-production data. The fact that there are increasing returns due to a learning curve means that they will be selling below their initial unit costs even if they are charging the same prices in all markets. Thus, they will be subject to antidumping duties. As has often been pointed out, the fully-allocated-cost standard is also inherently discriminatory against imports because it does not require domestic producers to sell above their costs.

While there are good reasons for questioning whether the sweeping nature of present antidumping laws makes good sense on fairness or economic grounds, it is unlikely that major changes can be made in the antidumping code during the Uruguay Round. The developing countries should press for some changes, however, particularly modifications to preclude antidumping laws being used to prevent market entry by new, potentially efficient producers. Perhaps providing new producers with a period of adjustment to reach efficient production levels before applying the antidumping laws (similar to the way that infant firms receiving government subsidies might not be subject to countervailing duties for a limited period), or tightening the injury standards in these cases would achieve this objective. Requiring those firms bringing antidumping charges to compensate those accused of dumping for the costs of the proceedings if the administering authority finds no sales at less than fair value may also reduce the frequency of this law being used to harass import competitors, especially those from developing countries.

Both the LDC and DC negotiators should request that the antidumping committee established under the code investigate how well antidumping laws have worked in the signatory countries since the code went into effect. The increasing complexity in the antidumping rules and procedures of many countries should be examined to determine if some simplification in procedures is appropriate, since some countries suspect that many of the new procedures are designed mainly to make it easier for firms to get general protection rather than to prevent dumping. The different criteria followed by the signatories in determining material injury should also be analyzed to assess the possibilities of establishing uniform criteria for all countries.

Increasing GATT Participation by the Developing Countries

Though both developed and developing countries will benefit in the long run from restoration of the MFN principle in safeguard actions, more detailed and realistic rules on subsidies, and changes in the antidumping code to prevent its use as a general protective device, the burden of adjusting in the short run will fall disproportionately on the developed countries, and they will be reluctant to agree to these changes unless they perceive that developing countries are making comparable concessions.

As noted earlier, the developed countries want the developing nations to relinquish some of their special privileges under the GATT and to increase their participation in the framework of responsibilities under the Agreement. The key GATT article granting special privileges to the LDCs is Article XVIII. It permits these countries to adopt protective and other measures to implement their development programs and to apply quantitative restrictions for balance-of-payment purposes on a more or less indefinite basis. With these provisions in effect, the DCs see little chance of securing meaningful reductions in barriers to the LDCs' markets through GATT mechanisms.

The LDCs are being forced, during bilateral negotiations with the DCs, to give up their special privileges without gaining much in return. This suggests the possibility that the LDCs may agree to modifications in Article XVIII which bring the responsibilities of the more advanced developing countries closer to those of the DCs as part of a negotiating package in which the DCs agree to a strengthening of GATT rules on safeguards, subsidies, and dumping.

Developing countries could also make a concession within the framework of this negotiating package to bind their low levels of protection on capital goods and technically sophisticated intermediate inputs. These have been low because of their importance to the development programs of the LDCs, with their low skill levels and inadequate capital stock to produce such goods efficiently themselves. But as their development proceeds, there will be increasing domestic pressures in the LDCs to substitute domestic production for imports of many of these items. As previous negotiating experience has demonstrated, it is easier to obtain a commitment for low protective levels before there is significant domestic production than after vested domestic interests have been established.

Mutual benefits can also be gained by further reductions in the DCs' import barriers on manufactured goods. A recent UNCTAD study (Sampson 1986) indicates that reducing U.S., EC, and Japanese tariffs to zero on an MFN basis will increase LDC exports to these countries by 2.8 percent, even if such sensitive items as textiles, apparel, iron, steel, and footwear are excluded. Reducing both tariff and nontariff barriers on these items raises LDC exports by 5.4 percent.

Both the DCs and LDCs have much to gain from liberalization of trade in textiles, apparel, and services, but many DCs fear that severe adjustment problems will accompany liberalization of textile and apparel trade, while many LDCs fear that they will lose if trade in services is liberalized. This suggests the possibility of "concessions" by the DCs when the Multi-Fibre Arrangement is renegotiated in return for "concessions" by the LDCs with regard to services trade.

Conclusion

The negotiating environment for achieving increased access to world markets for manufactured goods has changed dramatically in the last 10 to 15 years. No longer are the DCs willing to open their markets to manufactures from the LDCs without securing meaningful concessions in return. Indeed, the adjustment problems caused by the increase in exports from the LDCs and industrial countries such as Japan have led to widespread support in the EC and the United States for withdrawal of the special concessions made to the LDCs and encouragement to open their markets much more to achieve a current balance of concessions. The EC and the United States are already pursuing this goal with some success through bilateral negotiations with the LDCs. In addition, by negotiating VERs and other country-selective import restrictions, and by making it easier for domestic industries to gain protection through antidumping and countervailing actions, a number of industrial trading nations are curtailing access to their domestic markets for manufactured goods.

To achieve a more balanced and mutually beneficial opening of markets, the developing countries should press in the Uruguay Round for a strengthening of GATT rules on safeguards, subsidies, and dumping. In return for rules that restrict the DCs' ability to avoid adjustment in declining industries and use unfair trade laws for protective purposes, the LDCs should consider accepting changes in GATT rules that would require them to assume responsibilities closer to those carried by the DCs. They should also consider balancing concessions in the area of traded services for concessions by the DCs in the textile and apparel field.

Comment   *Patrick Low* *

DR. LOW: I think there are three important respects in which Professor Baldwin's paper is useful. First, it highlights how the international trading environment has changed, particularly since the Tokyo Round, and how developing countries now face much greater pressure than before to participate more actively in negotiations and in the trading system. A failure to do so risks leaving developing countries on the sidelines. Even worse, developing countries could find themselves facing growing discrimination against their exports, with the obvious negative consequences for growth that this would imply.

The second useful feature of the paper is that it pitches the analysis in terms of the kinds of bargains that might be struck in negotiations. This is a very practical approach. The process of trying to construct bargains attractive to the participants in the negotiations is something that has not yet begun in any explicit way in the Uruguay Round. At the moment there is a set of 15 ostensibly independent negotiating groups, each addressing its own issues.

*Patrick Low is on leave from the GATT Secretariat. The views expressed here are his own and should not be attributed to the Secretariat.

Ideas about how these issues might meld into bargain sets can therefore be very helpful at this stage.

Third, it is useful to identify clearly, as Professor Baldwin does, the link that exists between safeguards on the one hand and antidumping and countervailing duty actions on the other. It may seem an obvious point, but the interrelationship between these two areas of "contingency" trade policy is important, but has received scant attention.

The central question in Professor Baldwin's paper is what would constitute a bargain for developing countries in the negotiations. In terms of what they would seek, the paper concentrates on safeguards and antidumping and countervailing duty issues. While there are naturally other matters of significance to developing countries in the negotiations, these are obviously crucial areas insofar as access to industrial country markets is concerned. In exchange for well-functioning and equitable rules in these areas, Professor Baldwin argues for greater discipline in developing country import regimes, specifically with respect to recourse to Article XVIII and tariff bindings.

Professor Baldwin's opposition to the use of discriminatory safeguard measures can only be endorsed. A formal departure, or more precisely a formalization of existing and future departures, from the most-favored-nation (MFN) principle in the area of safeguards would fundamentally change the nature of the trading system. The change would be entirely negative. In particular, it would significantly reduce the degree of security of market access available to small countries and small suppliers. It would increase the power over markets of sectoral pressure groups, of politicians and bureaucrats and, in general, reduce the potential for gains from trade. It would also, by its nature, tend to carry with it all the costs attendant upon import regimes which rely on quantitative restrictions, as it seems to be the case that, for the most part, selectivity in this context requires quantitative rationing.

In addition, the use of selective safeguard measures would be likely to result, over time, in the institutionalization of market sharing arrangements, perhaps going even further than the Multi-Fibre

Arrangement by generalizing sharing arrangements into third markets. Experience of institutionalized non-MFN sectoral arrangements, in particular the MFA, suggests that once such arrangements are in place, not only are they politically difficult to eradicate, but they tend to become more restrictive over time. Also, because they rely upon bargaining among bureaucrats and upon essentially political processes, they tend to be inherently unstable and therefore become independent sources of political costs, irrespective of their economic costs. For all these reasons, then, there is a strong presumption in favor of the maintenance of the MFN principle if trade is to be permitted to play its established role as a significant source of income generation and growth.

There remains, however, a need to define nondiscrimination more closely, and to distinguish between different kinds of departures from the MFN principle. In the absence of a clear understanding of the prerequisites of a multilateral trading system, in terms of the MFN principle, the debate becomes somewhat abstract and removed from the real world. In this respect, perhaps Professor Baldwin implies that regional trading arrangements and developing country preferences are hostile to the maintenance of a viable multilateral trading system. In a definitional sense, these arrangements obviously breach the MFN principle, but it is useful to try to distinguish between discriminatory trade practices which are designed to protect particular industries, and departures from MFN which might create greater opportunities for trade or increased levels of discipline with respect to particular trade rules.

It would be difficult to maintain, for example, that customs unions and free-trade areas, as envisaged under Article XXIV, would have to be outlawed in order to maintain the essence of multilateralism. As long as Article XXIV arrangements are controlled appropriately, there is no reason why they should be seen as intrinsically hostile to the system. A problem arises, of course, from the widely held view that Article XXIV disciplines have been largely ignored, and that these arrangements have resulted in unjustified discrimination of a protectionist nature against outsiders. This issue is currently being taken up in the Uruguay Round. Similar arguments might be constructed in favor of special and differential treatment for developing countries. Once again, however, it must be borne in mind that refinements of matters of principle, while perhaps inevitable in the real world, are potentially dangerous. Unless the relevant rules are clear and are respected, these refinements can bring the system down rather than shoring it up.

Turning to more specific suggestions in the paper, the idea of trading off selectivity against compensation and retaliation under the safeguard provisions of Article XIX, which has been proposed before in some of the literature, is well worth exploring. In fact, this idea has found its way into the formal negotiating process. There is a proposal before the negotiation group on safeguards which foresees the possibility of waiving compensation or retaliation for a specific time period after a safeguard action has been taken, provided, of course, that it is an MFN action. An interesting question would then be what happens at the end of that time period. It may not be very helpful if at the end of the period, instead of terminating the measure, the whole debate about compensation and retaliation is resumed. The pressure for a discriminatory approach may simply have been deferred. In such cases it might be better to think in terms of Article XXVIII, to recognize that safeguard actions are not always short-lived and may reflect structural changes, and thus to envisage the possibility of tariff renegotiations in the event that a safeguard action is not terminated. This, of course, presupposes that all tariffs are contractually bound at maximum levels.

Turning to the issues of subsidies and dumping, and countervailing and antidumping duties, Professor Baldwin correctly identifies a serious practical problem in this area. It is how to ensure that measures designed to guard against unfair trade practices, which are politically necessary and theoretically defensible, are not used as protective devices, and what is worse, as discriminatory protective devices which can substitute for safeguard measures. This is an extremely difficult area. In certain ways, the Tokyo Round codes on subsidies and countervailing duties and on antidumping have complicated matters, and in the view of some, actually made them worse. The codes provide guidance through a wealth of technical and procedural detail, but many differing interpretations remain on points of substance and procedure.

One problem is the degree of discretion enjoyed by administrators. Another has been the unwillingness of some countries to align their domestic legislation with internationally agreed rules. Unfortunately, the Tokyo Round codes introduced the notion of price undertakings, both with respect to antidumping and antisubsidy actions. The idea is that if a country is threatened by one of these actions, it is legitimate to volunteer a price undertaking or to accept the suggestion of the importing country in exchange for the termination or suspension or the action in question. It is even worse in the case of countervailing duty actions, where undertakings can also take the form of quantitative limitations on exports. Part of an attractive bargain for developing countries would certainly be a clarification and improvement of disciplines in these areas.

Another point on the issue of subsidies, not raised by Professor Baldwin, but where developing countries have particular grounds for concern, is that present practices, if not the rules themselves, effectively prevent developing countries from correcting the antiexport biases of their industrial development policies. In other words, developing countries sometimes find themselves unable to neutralize the effects of their import regimes on their export prices without facing countervailing duty actions. The problem can arise irrespective of the degree of rationality or efficiency of the industrial development policies concerned. Very little work has been done on this, and it is an important issue deserving attention.

The idea mentioned by Professor Baldwin of binding subsidies in a manner similar to that in which tariffs are bound is certainly worth exploring. One question which springs to mind, however, is how easy would it be to ensure nondiscriminatory and transparent bindings of subsidies. It would probably be more difficult than has been the case with bindings on tariffs.

On the other side of the bargain, the question of increased discipline in developing country import regimes touches on Article XVIII, and particularly Article XVIII(b), which deals with balance-of-payments issues, and Article XVIII(c), which is the infant industry exception. There are already position papers on the negotiating table about how to introduce more rigor into the GATT's balance-of-payments provisions. A difficulty with Article XVIII(c) is that it is scarcely ever invoked because the rules relating to infant industry protection are more stringent than those concerning the balance of payments, and the latter have in practice been used to cover the former.

An additional question of relevance, mentioned by Professor Baldwin, is the possibility that developing countries could undertake additional tariff bindings. It is important to distinguish between bindings and binding levels. In the first instance, an offer by developing countries to bind more or less at any level might be considered a useful contribution. In this case, the level of the bindings would be for later consideration. An example of why this distinction is important is that under Article XVIII(c), it makes a significant difference whether or not an item is bound when restrictions are imposed on imports. There are several other instances as well where it is of fundamental importance whether or not a tariff is bound.

An issue not raised by Professor Baldwin, but which will be important in the negotiations is what strategy developing countries should adopt with respect to the possibility of the establishment or refinement of rules via the so-called code approach which was developed in the Tokyo Round. Implicit in this approach, which establishes rights and obligations applying only to code signatories, is the notion of conditional MFN. Conditional MFN should not be confused with the more general question of selectivity, although the approach nevertheless carries the risk that discrimination can be practiced against specific countries for protectionist ends. This is one reason why many developing countries oppose the code approach. However, pressures in the negotiations will probably militate towards the establishment of codes in certain areas, and this argues for active participation from developing countries to influence the nature and content of any such codes.

Finally, as Professor Baldwin acknowledges, any serious search for bargains would eventually require a more detailed examination of many other issues which have been included in the negotiations, and perhaps some which have not. In this connection, the possibilities of coalition formation among groups of countries warrant consideration. These possibilities, some of which have begun to emerge in the negotiations, are fundamental to any analysis of strategies available to developing countries.

Discussion

DR. CONYBEARE: I had a question for Professor Baldwin about something he didn't really raise in his paper, but I think is important in negotiations, and that is the question of whether free trade for developing country manufacturers is in the interest of the United States or is it just a disguised form of foreign aid; and if it is the latter, then wouldn't it be more efficient just to write them a check and save all those transactions costs?

I wouldn't have raised this except that you began your paper by citing the new strategic trade theory, and you said that this new theory (which emphasizes increasing returns to scale) means that free trade in manufactured goods is even more important for developing countries than we had thought before, and I agree with that.

Unfortunately, the corollary is that if you believe in the strategic trade theory, then preventing free trade in manufactured goods is now even more important for the United States and other developed countries which already have these increasing returns to scale industries.

So I think the advent of this new strategic trade theory bodes ill for the developing country arguments for free trade in manufactured goods because it very forcefully raises the question of whether or not free trade in these goods is good for the United States.

DR. WHALLEY: Is the system we now have likely to produce liberalization of trade and other policies by the governments which comprise it, such that each will be better off than it is now or would otherwise be?

It seems that the governments of both developed and developing countries are providing, by their practices, negative answers to this question. Within and between each of these two broad groups, bilateral negotiations are in ascendance and addressing issues which are deemed to be either inadequately addressed by, or exceptions to, the GATT.

Insofar as this negative answer is illustrated by bilateral negotiations between governments of developing and developed countries, I believe it is a consequence of the GATT possessing an institutional incongruity that is perhaps inescapable—that would be likely to characterize *any* set of rules intended to govern trade policies of so disparate a universe of governments and countries as exist on this planet. In a nutshell, the GATT is an MFN-based system, but the nondiscrimination and other good sense of most-favored-nation treatment of one another is less applicable to developed–developing country negotiations than to those confined to developed countries.

Small country negotiations with large countries are thwarted by the MFN rule because anything they might gain in the way of special treatment would have to be generalized to all other countries in the system. Governments of developing countries are not unsympathetic to this quandary; it accounts for their promotion of S&D, special and differential treatment of their interests both within and outside the GATT. Because of the inherent incompatibility between a rule of MFN and that of S&D, burgeoning bilateral negotiations would be surprising only in their absence.

I believe that the proliferation of bilateral quota instruments outside of the formal system provides commentary on the adequacy, or inadequacy, of the system itself, while also giving increased scope for reciprocal bargaining by developing countries.

Finally, I hope my remarks are not construed as anti-MFN or GATT. Quite the contrary. Instead, candid recognition of their limits encourages what I deem to be more practical questions. How, for example, might bilateral negotiations be structured and/ or interrelated in such a way as to strengthen the capacity for multilateral negotiations, including those within the GATT, to benefit their participants?

DR. MARES: I know that there is a concern to make GATT more relevant to a world in which we have increasing protection, but I think that in making it more relevant, we will actually be undercutting a lot of what GATT was attempting to do.

Particularly in the case of compensation, I think that if we remove the compensation/retaliation aspects, we will actually weaken the trade system by undercutting national-level supports for the international liberalization movement. I think that has impacts in two ways.

First, the mobilization and collective action of antiprotection groups at the national level is probably strengthened by the possibility of losses to them accepted by negotiators in order to protect another group, and so that is the domestic politics side.

Second, we have to remember that the international trade regime isn't something that just responds to international rules. It is very much a product of national trade politics, and if we undercut those domestic supports for liberalization, then we might find ourselves in a worse position.

DR. MORSS: I just wanted to talk briefly about technologies. There has been no real discussion about the very exciting new technologies and their implications for trade policies. The microprocessor is certainly the first thing that comes to mind. There are new materials, there are new combustion technologies, and we talked this morning about the biotechnologies. As a generalization, it can be said that these new technologies are labor and commodity saving.

This increases my concern about the idle-capacity fear, the fear of idle capacity as a disincentive to negotiating sincerely for free trade. We all went to the same schools and learned the same neo-classical welfare principles about maximizing welfare through free trade. I recently reviewed the assumptions underlying that welfare maximizing paradigm. Today, those assumptions are not valid.

Professor Baldwin recognizes this and says we have two options: we either look for another welfare paradigm, or we assert the assumptions are valid enough so we can continue to crusade for free trade through these various negotiating rounds. Professor Baldwin prefers the latter option.

I come out somewhat differently from Professor Baldwin. I look across the board and I don't see much free trade in the world, and I do see this great concern for employment. From this, I conclude that we have set ourselves up for another round of trade wars and protectionism. In such circumstances the incentives for pursuit of free-trade policies do not exist.

I just came back from Korea which has been moving ahead at a 35 percent export growth rate. Incidentally, this is a heavily subsidized export growth rate. We talk about the Asian Rim countries as outwardly-looking, which means they heavily subsidize exports.

Canada recently went after Hyundai for dumping. I don't know if that was the term they used, but what they came up with was a 40 percent subsidy. That means that the $6,000 Hyundai, which I think has definitely won the American markets, is being subsidized to the extent of 40 percent. I looked into this matter quite carefully. The Canadian claim was based on cost data, and not on a comparison of Hyundai prices in Canada and Korea.

In today's less-than-full-employment world, I find it most rewarding to think about future trade policy behavior in terms of nations trying to maximize employment. I then try to see if we can work towards free trade, or something like that, with this sort of national goal in mind.

What that means is to sacrifice a lot of efficiency because the primary concern of the people who are negotiating is employment and loss of employment, and not efficiency.

MS. SEIVER: I get the impression from the discussion this morning that people are automatically putting countervailing duty and antidumping actions in a protectionism slot. Certainly LDCs do, but if you take it as "leveling the playing field," it is not as protectionist—it is trying to make competition a little more equal. Maybe we shouldn't automatically call that protectionism.

The comment that these actions, especially in the United States, have increased so greatly is certainly true. But I think you have to consider that maybe the U.S. business community is getting a little more sophisticated in understanding the laws, and lawyers are getting a little more aggressive. Also, the fact that these cases are brought to the Department of Commerce doesn't mean that they are always upheld.

MR. GALLAGHER: I would like to comment on what Professor Morss said. It is very disturbing to me. The idea of a trade-off between efficient use of resources and employment wasn't something that I learned about in neoclassical economics and haven't seen contradicted yet.

The idea of a 40 percent subsidy on Hyundais to Canada seems to be quite a boon for the Canadians, that the Koreans are willing to subsidize Canadian consumption. Certainly it seems to me that export subsidies, unless they are corrections of distortions, have not in general improved the employment circumstances of the economies providing these subsidies.

I am not sure that the case is being made clear. This should be at least over a medium term, there should not be a contradiction between comparative advantage and free trade. That should not be in conflict with full-employment policies, and I do not see how it fits in there.

DR. KRUEGER: I think we are getting off the track on that one. We started by saying that our objective today was to talk about what possibilities there were for the international trading system in terms of the negotiations, and while there may be other theories of trade and so forth, I think that there is enough empirical evidence that the open system is beneficial to developing countries. I don't think we ought to ask, will they do it? I think we ought to ask what possibilities there are for getting there.

DR. MICHALOPOULOS: I have one comment on the subsidy issue. I think we have to be very careful about identifying subsidies that the developing countries are imposing because an awful lot of these subsidies are imposed to offset protection that is imposed by the same governments on imports and other kinds of taxes in their own internal economy, as well as to offset overvaluation of their exchange rate. Such subsidies have a different impact on international trade, but this kind of an issue has not been dealt with in the GATT at all. It is outside of the consideration that the GATT normally gives to the subsidy issue.

The other point that I wanted to discuss is the following: What is the proper emphasis that should be given to negotiations about the system and the setting up of mechanisms which improve the safeguard code, the subsidies code, countervailing questions, and so forth, versus negotiations which attack existing protection in the industrial countries in the manufacturing area which has been taken completely outside of the GATT context.

How do you get existing protection in the industrial countries reduced in addition to how you reform the system so that new protection is not imposed. I think the balance of those two issues needs to be very carefully addressed in the context of the negotiations.

MR. SPOSATO: I think the paradigm in question here is the precondition that the world economy would be in full employment. Without a world economy in full employment, specialization and trade advantages of free trade cannot go forward. They will be blocked by underemployment.

Nevertheless, I think the solution of trying to protect vested interests in a world economy which is not in full employment is not one which the leading industrial nation can take on. It is one which we may profit from but maybe not even in a profit-optimization situation.

I think we have to take the lead in pushing for a free-trade system, but also keep in mind that for the benefits to accrue, it does require a world economy in full employment. The problem we have, in terms of the negotiations and making these solutions palatable as the chair has suggested, is that labor unions especially see that in this situation of non-full-employment, some of their constituents are going to lose out.

We do have labor laws, however, which attempt to protect American labor from unfair practices overseas in countries which prevent unionization, which exploit workers in some ways. There are laws affecting our trade legislation in this regard. I think this is an important safeguard. Labor is important.

The ultimate benefits have to accrue to citizens of the world, and I think perhaps suggestions that these laws also be incorporated within the GATT in terms of acceptance of the benefits of the GATT may be a condition which will make negotiations much more palatable for many constituencies around the world.

MS. JOHNSON: In shaping U.S. strategies to achieve economic liberalization through GATT, we will be faced with concerns that appear to be in conflict and irreconcilable. These concerns are making maximum use of free-trade channels as a way to take advantage of efficiencies of technology, on the one hand, and finding ways to alleviate the worries of politicians about loss of wages and jobs by workers, on the other.

Since the issue of efficiency versus work force size and pay is going to be an underlying dilemma in international fora, would it not be useful for the United States to encourage persons taking part in those meetings to consider the advantages of widescale adoption of employee stock ownership plans or ESOPs as a practical step for addressing the dilemma. That is, homeland companies that accept and employ labor-saving technologies can make it possible for workers, through stock ownership via ESOPs, to have a stake in the additional profits to be realized by use of those technologies.

DR. ORDEN: I was interested, Professor Baldwin, in the section in your paper on subsidies, and I want to go back to our discussion in the agricultural area and then see if there is anything similar going on in the manufacturing area.

Although we haven't had much progress in the agricultural negotiations and, in fact, agriculture has generally been considered to be the dragging area in trade liberalization, in this Round there is quite a recognition by most of the traders that we need some sort of comprehensive measure that will bring together all the various domestic policies that countries use and the specific trade policies they use that affect agricultural trade.

The measure that has been kicked around is called PSEs, producer subsidy equivalents, which were mentioned earlier. Roughly speaking, a PSE is simply a measure of how much support the agricultural sector, or a specific crop, is getting in a country. The OECD has computed PSEs and compared them among countries.

In the proposals that have been tabled in Geneva several countries have mentioned PSEs and there has been a lot of discussion of whether we can use these PSEs, can we actually believe these numbers enough to use them for trade negotiations.

I think the best recognition of how important that discussion has become is in the Japanese proposal. If you will give a minute to read just a paragraph from it or a couple of sentences from it, they have a last part, part three, titled "Other Remarks," and the first section is on comprehensive aggregate measurement which is the PSEs.

They say the following: "In implementing the above proposal, there is no need for a comprehensive aggregate measurement of levels of protection and support. The producer subsidy equivalent developed by the OECD . . . is not designed to measure nor compare the level of protection to agriculture in respective countries."

So comparative measurement of support to agriculture has become a big enough issue for the Japanese to deny that we should use the OECD measure, while some others are pushing for them fairly strongly.

What I am interested in is whether there is any movement in manufacturing sectors to think about a comprehensive measure of the protection that an industry is getting that takes into account both the domestic and the specific trade-related impacts and to compare these measures among countries?

Response
Robert E. Baldwin

DR. BALDWIN: Let me respond to some of the points Patrick has made. He is right in saying that I usually am talking to groups who may not appreciate all the subtleties of the differences between the various concepts, but, to make my position clear, I am not opposed to regional agreements.

I continue to hope that regional agreements may be a route to liberalization. It is an encouraging sign that the Community has been willing to take in new member countries. Also, I think it is probably true that the Canadian–U.S. agreement has led to our taking some initiatives toward a liberalizing U.S.–Mexican agreement and that is all to the good.

But I have some concern as to whether the Community's liberalization will be complete and whether it will be a group that anyone who wants to can join. Many of its members' links are geopolitical, and I doubt if a country like Canada could get in or that they would allow the United States to enter the group.

One often hears that the Community has to have a five percent tariff, that is the cement that holds the Community together, and other such notions. This unwillingness to liberalize completely concerns me but this view is not too widely held yet and for the time being, these agreements on balance seem to have a positive effect so I would favor them, and also, the conditional codes.

What did we used to call the group in GATT that would assume higher responsibility?

DR. LOW: GATT-Plus.

DR. BALDWIN: I thought that GATT-Plus was an acceptable idea, and I would support the conditional code route. Though not everyone accepts them now, the way is left open for anyone to join in time; I think that is a reasonable position.

You said that you would not formally give up the MFN approach and I strongly agree.

I am prepared to accept other devices, such as preferences, as not violating the basic purpose of the MFN principle. It is like reverse discrimination. There is a big difference between preferences and discrimination, and preferences are a form of an advantage given to some groups that have been disadvantaged.

I am even prepared to say that in some cases reclassifying some items for tariff purposes is legitimate. It is fairly clear that in the automotive industry not all automobiles are alike. I suspect you could have separated out some of the high-priced European cars and introduced high duties on all low-priced cars without any hassle.

Remember the old chicken war back in the Kennedy Round. We retaliated against the Germans for their policy on chickens by establishing a separate tariff classification for Volkswagen cars.

So I don't mean to imply that I am against preferences or against free trade areas. I think they are now working for general liberalization, but I think that giving up the MFN principle, particularly in safeguards, would be very bad and lead to more protectionism.

John raised the question of whether free trade is in the interests of the United States. Some of the new trade literature sounds as if it is in our interest not to allow free trade.

Paul Krugman has an interesting article in *Economic Perspective* entitled, "Is Free Trade Passé?" in which he, one of the proponents of the so-called new policy, comes out for free trade, interestingly, on political economy grounds.

As you know, some are advocating the use of this new policy, using protection or subsidizing for strategic purposes, but you don't know what game is being played, whether it is Cournot-Nash or Bertrand or some combination, so you therefore don't know whether you should introduce a tax or a subsidy.

I have a feeling that the underlying problem is that we have never been able to articulate a good dynamic argument for free trade. We see in recent history that those developing countries that have opened up have achieved significant growth.

Although we have abundant historical evidence suggesting the benefits of liberalization, to convince people these days you have to be able to formulate a position in rigorous theoretical terms. Those who can successfully model the dynamic case for liberalization are going to go down in history with Ricardo.

In safeguard cases I would rather keep the MFN principle and give up the compensation requirement, even though this is not the perfect solution. You are giving up one antiprotection factor, but by gaining MFN you get political pressures against protectionism being exerted by other countries.

Marilyn Seiver mentioned the level playing field; she is right, but many times I think that some selective subsidies actually make the playing field more level. Just to assume that any subsidy makes it unlevel and therefore must be countervailed is not right.

We know there are some good economic arguments for subsidies. You may need subsidies to correct domestic distortions that exist. We should have recognized in the subsidies code the legitimacy of subsidies for offsetting certain distortions.

But, of course, there are also many subsidies that are straight trade-distorting mercantilistic actions, and I approve of tough countervailing actions by government against these subsidies.

I think, however, that in some cases countervailing actions have gone too far and are being used improperly for protective purposes.

We have to guard against this trend because we know that there is strong domestic political pressure that tends to work in that direction.

Regarding Costas' point about attacking existing protection and reforming the system and which of those should come first, my argument is that you will not get the rollback until you get some sort of agreement on these other matters. I doubt if we will get any significant rollback without resolving the problems that led to the increased protection in the first place.

I don't think rollback or standstill agreements are going to go very far by themselves. I don't hear much about rollback these days and would like to know what progress is being made in the Uruguay Round to carry out this objective. I suspect that it is going to be tied in with progress on other fundamental issues. Once we get such progress we will then rollback some of the new quantitative restrictions, perhaps by turning them into tariffs, and then gradually reducing these tariffs.

Regarding your point about whether we have aggregate measures of protection, you remember in the Tokyo Round one suggested approach was to hold sector negotiations in which we would look at the subsidies, the tariffs, and other trade-distorting measures in a sector, put them together into an aggregate measure of protection, and then use this for negotiating purposes. That didn't seem to go very far. I am not sure why it never got off the ground but the notion was to find out all the different trade-distorting measures in a sector, measure them in tariff-equivalent terms and then negotiate a reduction in this net measure of protection.

It was hard to negotiate in this manner. First, in sectors, you have to have roughly the same level of net protection among countries to achieve reciprocity. That is hard to find.

But I am all in favor of trying sector negotiations and certainly of efforts to determine the extent of net protection in various industrial sectors. This would help deal with the other point I mentioned, namely, that maybe on balance a subsidy instead of being a distortion, is setting off another distortion.

DR. KRUEGER: Patrick, do you want to just say a few words about roll back or anything else you would care to get into with respect to the discussion?

DR. LOW: To take up the question just raised about whether there is something like a PSE in the manufacturing sector, in the negotiations this has not been made explicit. However, some countries want a negotiating approach which would take tariffs and non-tariff measures and try to negotiate them together. Such an approach might call for the development of a measure akin to a PSE.

As far as standstill and rollback are concerned, it must be recognized that these are rather odd concepts. In crude terms, standstill is a promise to be good, and rollback is an admission of having been bad and a promise to reform. Such undertakings obviously have political significance, but they do not sit easily with the contractual obligations that underlie the General Agreement. A seeming lack of commitment to the undertakings has been a source of complaint among some participants in the negotiations.

So it is not all that surprising that we have actually seen no roll back actions. There have been discussions, there have been notifications, there has been no admission by any participant in the negotiations that they have measures to roll-back. If something does happen, it will be a politically negotiated deal, but it certainly isn't ripe yet.

Development, Trade, and International Organizations

Introduction

The evolution of the international economy in the 1980s has had a profound, but differentiated, impact on developing countries' trade policies and their approach to participation in the global trading system. There is widespread consensus that expanded international trade is essential both for long-term development and for the resolution of the persistent debt-servicing difficulties currently faced by many developing countries. Increased protection in industrial countries' markets through arrangements that violate the letter or the spirit of the GATT, combined with depressed commodity prices, has caused concern about the dangers of an increasingly hostile trading environment. At the same time, a widening recognition that their own restrictive trade policies inhibited exports and economic growth has led many developing countries to undertake programs of trade liberalization and rationalization, often with the assistance of the World Bank and the IMF.

The launching of the Uruguay Round of multilateral trade negotiations under the GATT in 1986 came in the midst of the debt crisis and slower growth in the developing world compared to the previous two decades. It also came at a time when both industrial and developing countries felt that the GATT, the key institution underpinning the multilateral trade system, had been severely weakened by restrictive trade actions in areas largely outside its effective control. The Punta del Este Declaration launching the Round seeks to reverse this trend through negotiations aimed at liberalizing trade, as well as strengthening the institutional role of the GATT. But this agreement should not obscure considerable differences among member countries, especially developing ones, in their views about the future role of the GATT and their participation in it.

To make progress towards a better world trading environment will therefore require concentrated effort. In this effort international financial institutions have an important role, notably the World Bank and the IMF. This paper addresses two questions: First, what role can the international institutions play in promoting the expansion of developing countries' trade? Second, what approaches can developing countries take to maximize the benefits to their trade through their participation in these international institutions?

The paper starts with an overview of the links between trade and development. This is followed by some observations about the institutional setting and the approaches of the GATT, the World Bank, and the IMF to promote development through trade. Next, alternative approaches to developing countries' participation in the Uruguay Round and the GATT are analyzed. The final section examines potential linkages of the three institutions in support of expanding developing countries' trade.

Trade and Development

There is abundant evidence based on the experience of the last thirty years that economic growth in developing countries is closely related to their export growth.[1] Export growth in turn is only partly the result of demand-side factors deriving from the economic performance and trade policies of OECD countries which constitute the developing countries' main markets. Increasingly the evidence suggests that differences in the export growth performance of developing countries can be explained by their own policies and attitudes towards international trade. When world trade was expanding rapidly, as it did for example from 1960 to 1973, developing countries' trade and economic growth was somewhat greater than in the period from 1973 to 1981, irrespective of their own policies. But in each period the performance of countries with more effective, outward-oriented international economic policies was, on average, far superior to those with inward-looking, heavily protected trade regimes.[2]

Successful export performance requires policies which provide adequate incentives for investment in the export sector or efficient import substitution and ensure that these incentives will be steadily maintained. This involves a broad set of specific policies. First and foremost, it requires an exchange rate policy under which the returns to tradeables adequately reflect the value to the economy of the foreign exchange earned or saved. Second, it requires that the trade regime—which includes such specific policies as tariffs, quotas, exchange restrictions, and taxes of all kinds on imports— approach neutrality, in that it does not discriminate against production for exports compared to production for the domestic market. Although in principle such neutrality can be achieved through a combination of policies which tax or restrict imports and subsidize exports, in practice, the design of effective tax cum subsidy policies is so complex and open to distorting political action that it is rarely possible.[3] Thus neutrality can best be achieved through minimum and undifferentiated barriers to trade. Third, investment in exports and efficient import substitutes involves ensuring access to capital—

both from abroad and domestically. This in turn requires limiting the absorption of savings in public sector deficits (on current account) and the avoidance of capital flight by confidence-creating economic management.

Recent analyses show that countries which came closer to pursuing such policies attained faster growth in both exports and GNP, had higher rates of domestic savings and experienced greater gains in total factor productivity.[4] It is important to emphasize that the link between effective policies to expand exports and overall economic performance is not a phenomenon that characterized simply a few economies—such as the so-called Gang of Four (Korea, Taiwan, Hong Kong, and Singapore). The contrast in overall economic performance is still striking when one compares the performance of moderately outward-oriented economies, such as Brazil and Thailand, to that of inward-oriented economies, such as Argentina and Tanzania. Moreover, countries which have pursued more open trade and exchange rate policies have been better able to keep export levels up throughout the shocks in the international economy of the last 15 years—even though their outward orientation has meant that the shocks they sustained were greater.[5]

This evidence gives some clues about the nature of the link of trade to development: It is not solely, or perhaps even mainly, a demand-driven link, whereby export growth stimulates incomes and output in the rest of the economy. Rather, effective participation in international trade permits economies of scale not open to small protected economies. By introducing greater market competition, it encourages a more efficient utilization of resources and greater growth in productivity in the whole economy. Moreover, open trading policies permit quicker adaptation to new technologies and greater flexibility in responding to international economic developments.

These lessons are gradually being understood by the governments of most developing countries. By the early fifties most developing countries had instituted a high degree of protection to promote industrial development through import substitution. It was thought that a temporary period of high protection would encourage the development of "infant industries," which would later on be able to compete internationally without the protection. Protective barriers and foreign exchange restrictions also spread when, as a consequence of overly ambitious development efforts, developing countries encountered balance-of-payments difficulties but were unwilling to adjust the exchange rate or persevere with effective macroeconomic adjustment.

At different points in time during the 1960s and 1970s, most developing countries found themselves saddled with overall highly protective regimes, which contained large and haphazard variations in the degree of protection by activity and sector.[6] These regimes did not save foreign exchange but only resulted in a significant anti-export bias, and in a misallocation of resources with adverse effects on overall growth.

As countries recognized the pitfalls of these inefficient import substitution strategies, they attempted to rationalize and liberalize their trade regimes.[7] But they encountered a number of difficulties. First, trade liberalization frequently foundered on the rocks of ineffective macroeconomic, and especially exchange rate, policies. In the absence of sound policies the reform efforts were not credible, and in turn, precipitated responses by the private sector that contributed to their early abandonment. All too often, exchange rates were kept well below those which would reflect market forces. Frequently, governments feared the tensions that would arise from higher prices for food and petroleum products, which are key imports in many countries, and postponed the exchange rate action which would have given the more efficient structure of incentives needed for growth. A second key reason why reduction of import controls has proved difficult is because these controls have resulted in substantial private profits through the spread of uneconomic "rent-seeking" activities, including the corruption of public officials and, more generally, have been the source of benefits used to keep political alliances intact.

These difficulties were compounded by the onset of the debt crisis in the 1980s. Developing countries faced mounting debt service obligations in the context of a deteriorating international economic environment. This environment was characterized by three key developments: First, declining primary commodity prices and deteriorating terms of trade for most developing countries; second, increased protection for manufactures by industrial countries and increased subsidies for their agricultural exports, both of which were undertaken through measures that contravened or bypassed their obligations under the GATT; third, reduced inflows of capital from private banks.

Faced with these balance-of-payments difficulties, many heavily indebted countries were tempted in the first instance to resort to trade and exchange controls to restrict imports. But when help was arranged through the Bretton Woods institutions, they resisted this impulse surprisingly well. This was undoubtedly due, in large part, to an understanding that resolution of the debt problem requires an expansion of imports rather than a contraction, and this expansion can only occur in the context of a growing international economy and expanding trade.

In this situation, the major trading nations have an obligation to examine what they can do to help forestall protectionism at home and to encourage policies in developing countries which promote adjustment with growth. Their role is both bilateral and multilateral in character. The growth performance and the market openness of industrial countries has, of course, a direct bearing on the export performance and balance-of-payments prospects of developing countries which remain, by and large, highly dependent on these markets. Success in recent efforts to improve macroeconomic policy coordination among the major industrial countries and to bring about more exchange rate stability, would thus have a direct positive impact on the economies of developing countries. Beyond that, the industrial countries can open their markets and provide both moral and financial support to the process of creating conditions favorable to policy reform in developing countries. With such support, confidence can be created that the incentives to invest in the export sector of developing countries will be maintained. Moreover, availability of resources will be essential to strengthen the hand of policymakers in developing countries committed to policy reform and thus give greater assurance that the often politically difficult process will be sustained.

The major trading nations also must take the lead in helping and strengthening multilateral institutions which can play an important role in supporting developing countries' own efforts. The institutions have a threefold role. First, they provide a framework for international rules that are supportive of developing countries' trade and development policies. Second, they often provide valuable technical assistance in designing policy reforms and strengthening domestic institutions that promote international trade and development. Third, the financial assistance they provide directly facilitates the pursuit of policies that promote trade and development. Even more broadly, the industrial countries' attitude in support of the multilateral institutions—the GATT, the IMF, and the World Bank—is bound to affect favorably the developing countries' own interest in influencing the direction in which the institutions will evolve in the future.

The Role of GATT, IMF, and the World Bank

Promotion of international trade has been a common concern both to the GATT and to the Bretton Woods institutions. The GATT had been envisaged to play the central role in trade through (a) the establishment of a set of international rules that would promote a multilateral trade system characterized by nondiscrimination, stability, and transparency in trade relations; trade controls under the system were expected normally be in the form of tariffs; and (b) the creation of a forum within which tariffs would be reduced progressively through negotiations on "a reciprocal and mutually advantageous basis."[8] The IMF was intended to ensure a stable international exchange rate system under the par value system and strict control over exchange restrictions so providing the essential environment for international trade to flourish. The World Bank, through its assistance to investment in infrastructure and other projects, was expected to help increase and diversify productive capacity thereby facilitating growth of international trade.

Over time these roles have evolved in ways not fully anticipated. In some respects they fell short of the initial hopes, but, in a broader perspective, they succeeded beyond the greatest expectations of their creators. The challenge at this stage is to take stock and find the strength to cope with the problems now emerging.

The GATT. The GATT achieved important success in reducing tariff barriers but, with respect to other barriers which have become increasingly significant, its role was somewhat circumscribed. For example, protection on agricultural trade was left intact to accommodate then existing U.S. legislation and agricultural support programs. And the rules, especially on nontariff barriers, were not backed by enforcement powers. The GATT Secretariat was small and could not on its own undertake surveillance of members' adherence to the agreed rules. Consequently any violations of such rules were expected to be notified to the GATT by other members.

GATT provisions also reflected the economic thinking and the institutional biases of the time. It appeared reasonable for example, in a system of fixed exchange rates, to permit all countries to impose temporary quantitative restrictions in response to balance-of-payment difficulties or loss of reserves (see GATT Article XII). Developing countries which faced balance-of-payments difficulties were given wider latitude to impose restrictions under Article XVIII(b). Similarly, the principle of infant industry protection for less developed countries was recognized, and trade restrictions consistent with it were also permitted under Article XVIII.

In the realm of trade liberalization, the principle of reciprocity embedded in Article XXVIII was used in successive rounds of GATT negotiations to reduce tariffs of industrial countries to very low levels for most commodities. Reciprocity proved useful as a means of mobilizing domestic political support for trade liberalization. It did so by encouraging the formation of domestic coalitions between exporters and consumers who gain from reductions in trade barriers and whose support is essential in countervailing the political power of producers with vested interest in protection. Although the reciprocity principle caters to the mercantilist perception that benefits from trade derive solely from export expansion while increases in imports entail only costs, its practical implementation led to significant trade liberalization and supported world economic expansion in the 1950s and 1960s.

While the industrial countries managed to reduce tariffs considerably, developing countries never participated as their equal partners in the GATT. In part, particularly for many of the smaller countries, this was due to institutional weaknesses making it difficult to participate in multilateral trade negotiations. But more generally it was due to a desire of most developing countries in the GATT, from its inception, to place themselves in the position of being allowed to rely on trade restrictions and protection in the interest of their trade and development needs.

To the extent that the original GATT articles failed to formally recognize their special status, the developing countries, in keeping with the protectionist trade policies to which most were committed, sought to incorporate rules for differential treatment in their favor on the occasion of subsequent amendments to the GATT or in the development of new rules of conduct in successive rounds of trade negotiations.[9]

Part IV of the GATT, introduced in 1965, provided that the developed countries did not require reciprocity for commitments made by them in trade negotiations to reduce or remove tariffs and other barriers to trade with less developed countries. This provision represented formal acknowledgment of the fact that reciprocity, as practiced in trade negotiations, often meant that individual developing countries with small markets had little to offer in return for reductions in the trade barriers of industrial countries. Thus, while developing countries were able to benefit from reductions in tariff barriers among industrial countries which were extended to them on an MFN basis under the GATT, they did not themselves engage in reciprocal tariff reduction negotiations. Consequently, at the end of the Tokyo Round, tariffs on items of importance to their trade were, on average, higher than on items of importance to industrial countries' trade.

The infant industry rationale was extended to exports in the Generalized System of Preferences (GSP) which was instituted following an UNCTAD initiative in 1968 and a GATT waiver in 1971. While providing for duty-free entry in industrial country markets of developing country products, the GSP excluded many products of special industrial importance to developing countries such as steel, textiles, clothing, and shoes. Notwithstanding Part IV of the GATT, the GSP benefits were implemented unilaterally by the preference-giving countries and could thus be withdrawn at any time. Following its establishment, the developing countries devoted considerable effort to making the GSP benefits permanent, with little success. Indeed, with growing protectionist pressures, preference-giving countries tended progressively to limit the scope of GSP benefits to developing countries.

The historical evolution of trade relations between developed and developing countries has thus been paradoxical. On the one hand, industrial countries, to a large degree, have accommodated many of the developing countries' demands in GATT and other forums for special and differential trade treatment, partly because it appeared to be a relatively costless way of securing developing countries' continued participation in the system. At the same time, however, it has been increasingly acknowledged that developing countries as a group do not benefit to a substantial degree from the preferential regimes they have formally secured for themselves. Moreover, developing countries' insistence on nonreciprocity in trade negotiations has encouraged their major trading partners to ignore their genuine concerns about the availability of access to industrial country markets on products of special importance to them.

On the other hand, industrial countries themselves increased their protection in a number of areas of actual or potential importance to the developing countries, such as steel, textiles, and clothing, often using nontariff barriers, such as voluntary export restraints (VER), orderly marketing arrangements, price monitoring, and a variety of other instruments incompatible with either the letter or the spirit of their GATT obligations. Sometimes countervailing and antidumping provisions in trade legislation were also used for protective purposes to restrict imports from developing countries. Moreover subsidization of agricultural exports by industrial countries has been extensive, and has proliferated.

The rise of this "new protectionism" in the industrial countries in the late 1970s and early 1980s has tended to weaken the GATT overall—after all, developing countries' trade restrictions were broadly considered "legal" under the GATT rules industrial countries themselves had acquiesced in! At the same time the rising importance of developing countries in international trade meant that industrial countries had a growing interest in reducing protection in developing countries. Thus while trade restraints on North-South trade have persisted, and in some cases increased, economic realities have increased greatly the rewards of liberalization. Mutual trade concessions could generate considerable support from both sides, if formulas can be devised to move forward.

The IMF and the World Bank. The Bretton Woods institutions, while not directly involved in trade negotiations, over time have had a large and growing interest in matters pertaining to world trade, particularly in creating conditions conducive to the growth of developing countries' trade. As the trade policies of many developing countries were in practice dominated by protracted balance-of-payments difficulties, the assistance given by the Bretton Woods agencies, through advice and financing, to overcome these problems were, on many occasions, much more important than specific GATT-related trade provisions in assuring the maintenance of trade flows. Thus the IMF, through its annual policy discussions with all members and provision of financing to overcome payment problems, has always had heavy responsibilities. The World Bank, through its wide-ranging project and nonproject lending activities, has had a systematic role in creating conditions for trade growth. And that role has been widened greatly by the recent development of policy-based lending which has frequently had a direct trade policy content.

In those countries with limited access to other forms of financing, the financing role of the agencies has been particularly powerful. International financial support can be extremely helpful in the transition from a heavily protected, inefficient productive structure to a more outward-oriented, dynamic economic structure which is more integrated into the international markets. Such a transition is fraught with difficulties: removal of import restrictions and other disincentives to exports, for example, may lead initially to an asymmetrical response, with imports rising much earlier than exports. The credibility of the reform package is greatly enhanced by the availability of external assistance to finance imports during this transition period.

Both the IMF and the World Bank combine their lending with an intensive policy dialogue with developing countries over the whole range of policies discussed earlier, which can contribute to expansion of trade. Compared to the GATT, these institutions have a substantially greater secretariat and, even more important, authority to exercise initiative in raising policy issues with individual members.

The system of annual consultations in the IMF, focusing on countries' macroeconomic policies in relation to the balance of payments, has ensured that individual efforts to progress towards the achievement of more open trading can be monitored and supported. For developing countries, these reviews have great importance, for they form the basis for policy discussions related to IMF lending. This lending requires assurances that exchange rate, fiscal, and monetary policies are pursued which will achieve an early balance-of-payments recovery. Moreover, in these lending agreements there is routinely a commitment from the borrowing government not to introduce import-restrictive measures for balance-of-payments reasons. The agreements normally involve a gradual phasing out of any existing exchange practices which are restrictive on imports.

The World Bank, through its project lending, has encouraged the development of production structures containing efficient export and import substitution industries that would be viable under international competition. Its involvement in an intensive dialogue with developing countries over matters pertaining to trade policy reform is more recent than that of the IMF and dates to the inauguration of the program of structural adjustment loans (SAL) in early 1980. In the last seven years, the Bank has approved SALs for 42 developing countries. These programs are designed to support wide-ranging economic reforms for the structural change essential to the restoration of economic growth. In almost all of these countries, the Bank has supported trade reform programs. In addition, the Bank has supported trade reform through sector loans—as in Mexico in 1986. The policy reforms supported usually are designed to reduce the bias of the trade regime against exports and to lower the level and variance in the patterns of protection. This frequently has involved recipient government commitments for phased reductions in quantitative barriers, as well as for reducing the range of tariffs over time. Since a key element in the viability of these reforms is the presence of a stable macroeconomic environment and an appropriate exchange rate, SALs and trade-related loans have almost always been provided to countries with an active IMF program.[10]

In order to promote structural change, and with the support of the World Bank and the IMF, a large number of developing countries have initiated trade policy reforms in the 1980s. Examples include Turkey, Korea, Chile, Mexico, Nigeria, and Morocco. It is instructive to note that these trade reforms, which almost always involve trade liberalization, have been undertaken by developing countries unilaterally without involving any binding commitments within the GATT and without any parallel concessions by industrial countries. The measures have usually been taken because governments have decided that they need to promote structural change by reducing the bias of existing trade regimes against exports. The availability of external finance through the World Bank or the IMF was typically only one of the arguments which strengthened the forces favoring trade reform within recipient governments.

Clearly, the liberalization efforts of developing countries, supported by the Bank and the IMF, are designed to be beneficial to these countries' development. However, the benefits that would accrue to them from such liberalization would be significantly increased if they were accompanied by improved access into industrial countries' markets. The two institutions have, as a consequence, frequently exhorted industrial countries to liberalize their trade because of the benefits that such liberalization would impart both on their economies and on those of developing countries. However, without the persuading strength of financing, the influence of these institutions has not been strong. The efforts of these institutions in support of a more liberal trade environment in the developing countries would be strengthened considerably, if industrial countries heeded their own advice—so frequently voiced in the deliberations of international institutions—to open up their own markets.

The Developing Countries and The Uruguay Round

The Setting. The launching of the Uruguay Round comes at a time when the developing countries attitudes towards GATT are changing. Recently a significant number of countries have decided to become GATT members. Of major importance in this change has been Mexico, where a decision to negotiate membership in GATT was an integral part of a comprehensive adjustment to the problems created by the debt crisis. The authorities have decided that GATT membership would be helpful in creating a more competitive economy leading to more diversified exports. Formal commitments have a role in containing protectionist pressures and fostering more open trade. The decision of China to reenter into effective GATT membership further shows the pervasiveness of the change. For China, it has been part of the strategy for an overall opening up of the economy. In still other cases the launching of the Uruguay Round has stimulated action to avoid being left out of potentially important negotiations.

The Uruguay Round provides a unique opportunity for worldwide trade reform, including changes to permit GATT to reflect new perceptions about the role of trade and development, as well as changes that strengthen GATT's institutional role in the surveillance of trade policy and the resolution of trade disputes. The Round provides an opportunity to evolve new practices affecting developing countries' interest in such important areas as nontariff barriers to their manufactured exports (e.g., textiles). Major issues also arise for them in the new areas of agriculture and services; they have a continuing interest in ensuring that a safeguard code is adopted which results in reduced use of VERs and other protective measures incompatible with GATT.[11]

In light of their stake in these negotiations, many developing countries have already been very actively involved. Some, like Brazil and India, have focused on limiting the scope of negotiations to the traditional area of trade and have been reluctant to place negotiations on services on the same footing.[12] Many others, including Colombia, Uruguay, the ASEAN group, Korea, China, and Mexico, have taken a broader view believing that any failure of these negotiations could lead to a continuing erosion of the multilateral trade system. A drift towards bilateral arrangements would predictably cause large losses in overall efficiency and in particular have very adverse effects on the smaller economies of the developing countries. Given the importance of the negotiations, the question is what strategies developing countries pursue to maximize their benefits from the Round.

Possible Strategies. The developing countries are severely constrained in their approach to negotiation by their diversity and by their small average size. Diversity makes it difficult to find common ground, while small economies make it imperative that they associate to lessen the intrinsic weakness of their bargaining position.

In the past, the main common ground has been found in the traditional approach of emphasizing special and differential treatment. But in current conditions a growing group of newly in-dustrializing countries are finding themselves drawn towards full participation in reciprocal bargaining with the industrial countries. This group finds that their offer to bargain will be taken seriously only if they are ready to forgo some of the differential treatment accorded in the past.

The resolution of these issues will not be easy. Nor will all developing countries follow a common strategy in the negotiations. Indeed their interests require that they do not. Yet, somehow, North-South trade issues must be resolved in this Round in ways that strengthen, rather than weaken, the coherence of the multilat-eral trading system. Clearly, it would be naive to believe, given the historical background, that all developing countries will be able or willing to coalesce around a strategy that involves rejecting the principle of special and differential treatment. Indeed, this princi-ple, already enshrined in GATT rules, may well be pressed and maintained even if it is not in the immediate economic interest of some of the more advanced developing countries. The decisions of individual developing countries may vary, and will likely become quite nuanced.

In deciding on these issues the more advanced countries will take into account the prospect that industrial countries are more likely to limit the special (GSP) benefits than expand them. Given the protectionist pressures within industrial countries as a conse-quence of competition in labor-intensive industries from a number of successful developing country exporters, it is unlikely that it would be politically feasible to generate the internal political con-sensus for more *favorable* treatment of developing countries. Indeed, the fear is that exactly the reverse may happen unless devel-oping countries are also prepared to reduce their own trade barri-ers. Consequently it seems probable that for this group of develop-ing countries, the reciprocal approach will seem attractive.[13] This will be the more so to the extent that these countries feel they can use this Round to extract concessions from industrial economies on market access in exchange for liberalization, which many developing countries may already have decided to offer.

For many of these countries the key trade problem is increased protection of industrial countries' manufactures; for others it is industrial countries' practices in agricultural trade. So most of these countries are likely to support the abstract principle of special and more favorable treatment, while actively negotiating on the issues that concern them in practice.

Undoubtedly, there are many other developing countries that will retain their traditional posture. Some of these will be countries which continue to favor highly protective trade regimes. Others are countries, especially in Africa, which, because of their economic size or export product range, do not believe the Uruguay Round offers significant opportunities for gain. This is regrettable as the trading system will be the better the more that participate.

Recognizing that developing countries individually have weak bargaining power and that a grand coalition is not practical except on abstract issues, the role of diverse coalitions among developing countries will probably be quite important. One kind of coalition will be based on issues that cut across industrialized and developing countries. One such issue is market access in agricultural trade, where the so-called Cairns Group includes a number of developing and industrial countries which are exporters of agricultural products. Such North-South groupings could in their negotiations allow divisions of interest among developing countries to emerge. For example, the Cairns Group will need to avoid too narrow an outcome to its pressures. An agreement which only reduces export subsidies on grains without equal advances on other items of importance to developing countries, such as sugar and beef, would be most unfortunate, as developing countries are net importers of grains.

Consequently there will be a variety of forms of coalitions among developing countries. Some, like the developing country coalition at Punta del Este led by Brazil and India, which forced a dual track in the negotiations on services, will be created in reaction to new proposals. Regional coalitions also will develop where interests are reasonably close—one of the strongest is likely to be the ASEAN countries, with the possible addition of Korea.

Key negotiating issues for the developing countries are certain to involve the development of rules on liberalization of nontariff barriers in specific sectors, such as textiles and clothing, steel, and shoes, which until now have escaped the liberalization process. The needed reorientation of the negotiating process will involve hard bargaining by the developing countries, and a readiness to give up the old approach of benefitting only, or largely, as free riders. Coalitions to lower nontariff trade barriers in favor of developing countries will not be easy to forge. In the Multi-Fibre Arrangement for example, developing countries have been somewhat divided because inefficient producers benefit from the higher prices possible on the restricted sales volume; by contrast genuinely low-cost producers have a lot to gain from a liberal regime based on tariffs. Thus, while all developing countries denounce the MFA in principle, in practice some have not pressed too hard for its replacement by a nondiscriminatory, tariff-based regime.

What can any group of developing countries offer in a negotiating process? This question is not simple. Developing countries often maintain widespread import controls and exchange restrictions. It is possible to negotiate "formula" cuts, where quantitative restrictions on a certain proportion of their imports could be eliminated over time in exchange for specific improvements in their access to individual sectors in industrial countries' markets. But such cuts may well be felt to be of dubious value given the persistence of payment problems in developing countries and the ease with which such problems can be invoked to impose trade restrictions under Article XVIII(b).

Consequently, those developing countries wishing to negotiate effectively will need to improve the security they offer by "binding" their tariff schedules and agreeing to tighter limitations on the use of balance-of-payments escape clauses contained in Article XVIII(b). In light of the flexibility of exchange rates now routinely available, reactions to payments problems should not take the form of trade or exchange restrictions. Reducing the scope or circumscribing actions to be taken under a balance-of-payments escape clause would not only make bargaining possible, it would also improve policy-making in the developing countries.[14]

Of course, willingness of any group of developing countries to negotiate on these lines presupposes, in part, a commitment by industrial countries to liberalize trade in a number of sensitive areas of key importance to the developing countries. For, while it is to the advantage of developing countries to rationalize and liberalize their trade regimes almost irrespective of the international environ-ment, it is extremely difficult politically to sustain such reform in the face of hostile trade action by industrial countries. Thus, to a large extent, success or failure of the Uruguay Round rests on the shoulders of the industrial countries.

Reluctance on the part of the industrial world will press devel-oping countries toward exploring the system of preferences for trade among developing countries, already under discussion for some time within UNCTAD. In principle, this is an attractive option, but in practice, it has proved virtually impossible to imple-ment in a meaningful way because of the diversity of interests of these countries and their unstable macroeconomic policies. More-over, even selective trade liberalization will be flawed from the outset if countries undertaking it continue to maintain an essen-tially inward-trading posture and remain unwilling to engage in substantial trade liberalization.

In principle, one of the most important issues for developing countries will be the development of an independent enforcement role for GATT management and Secretariat. With the broadening of negotiations from tariffs to nontariff barriers, and with the inclu-sion of agriculture and services, any agreements reached will need effective enforcement procedures far more than previous Rounds. The larger and richer countries undoubtedly will feel able to deal with this problem through bilateral negotiations. But for the weaker and smaller countries, the dangers are evident. They must have an impartial review mechanism, controlled by a stronger

GATT Secretariat, in which the rules are interpreted judicially. Of course for developing countries a dilemma will arise from concern that in practice the interpretation will not be impartial. Much more attention needs to be paid to this problem so that the technical basis for such a mechanism is developed more adequately. With progress here the prospects for developing country support would be greatly enhanced.

Bretton Woods Institutions and the GATT—Future Links

The world economy has been changed substantially since the launching of the last Round of trade negotiation in Tokyo in 1973. It is now much more integrated in all aspects of trade and finance. And the previous classification of countries has been bypassed by time. Many developing countries have grown to major importance in manufacturing trade. Income levels in many developing countries are now equal or exceeding those of the poorer new members of the EEC.

In these conditions, a major role of the Bretton Woods institutions has become the support of integration of developing countries into the international trading system. In this process, the ability of each country to produce tradeable goods efficiently has been crucial. The World Bank has frequently played—and will continue to play—a key role in this area by ensuring that adequate levels of financing are available to support movement towards greater integration of developing countries in the international trading system.

In this context it would be most encouraging if the trade liberalization measures undertaken by developing countries were to be recognized explicitly by industrial countries. Such recognition would be most effective if it took the form of credit usable towards partner-trade concessions in later GATT reciprocal negotiations. This idea, which is consistent with GATT procedures and has some minor precedents, was endorsed at the Development Committee meeting of April 1986 and raised at Punta del Este in September 1986.

Interestingly enough, most opposition to it in both forums came from developing countries because the concept of "credit" presupposes a willingness by developing countries to liberalize unilaterally. Industrial countries appeared willing to go along with the idea, provided trade reforms resulted in tariff bindings. Under the GATT system, trade concessions are of little value when they can be readily reversed. However, as noted earlier, developing countries, fearing balance-of-payments pressures have been reluctant to bind their tariff schedules (with some notable exceptions such as Chile and Mexico). Therefore, trade reforms with World Bank/IMF support, undertaken by developing countries which are members of GATT, are not notified to GATT and do not become their legal obligations.

Making the concept of credit operational is an issue deserving attention in the ongoing negotiations. Would it, for example, be feasible to provide credit and simultaneously to introduce time limited bindings, e.g., for five years? The bindings would become final after consultations between the GATT and member governments which would take into account balance-of-payments and development considerations. Whatever the final outcome, it is important to ensure that the Uruguay Round supports, rather than detracts, from the ongoing liberalization efforts of developing countries, and that to the extent feasible, World Bank/IMF support for trade liberalization is in a form which contributes to the negotiating process.

In examining the links between trade and finance the central issue is the degree of strengthening possible in the GATT as an institution. There is no doubt that trade-finance links would be much more manageable if the GATT was developed into an independent agency with a surveillance role on trade, much as the IMF has on international monetary issues. This would ensure that such issues as credit for trade reform in World Bank/IMF programs would be fitted into operating trade rules which have a much wider application. Moreover, the development of an independent GATT Secretariat with review authority on trade actions would greatly strengthen the surveillance role of international agencies now effectively limited to the annual consultations held by the IMF.

In light of the outcome of negotiations to strengthen the GATT, attention will also have to be paid to the role of the IMF. The IMF has, and will continue with, a direct role on exchange restrictions—a role of considerable importance on services if the new Round should successfully end with operating rules on this area. At present it also has responsibility for giving balance-of-payments judgments called for by the GATT. In the Uruguay Round, more reliance could be placed on IMF determinations, particularly if it was agreed to tighten the monitoring of any balance-of-payments escape clauses.

Finally, it will be appropriate for developing countries to investigate whether the Bretton Woods institutions could be used to strengthen their institutional capacity to negotiate. As noted, this capacity is very weak in many countries. The deficiencies could become even more glaring in this Round because of the complexity of the issues to be negotiated.

UNCTAD, GATT, and a number of other institutions have provided some technical assistance to developing countries in previous Rounds. The World Bank, with significant experience in institution building in developing countries and extensive analytical skills in trade, also initiated a modest program for the Uruguay Round. The Bank can undertake a more ambitious program. Such a role should be seen as reinforcing Bank support for developing countries' efforts to negotiate improved access to industrial countries' markets, rather than as unduly pressuring them to undertake liberalization they do not want.

Conclusions

Developing countries are currently faced with severe economic problems. For many, debt problems have curbed growth. For others, particularly in Africa, the structural problems inherent at present seem overwhelming. On top of this are the looming dangers involved in the process of correction of the trade imbalances of the largest three economies in the world. To meet this challenge, it is absolutely essential that trading practices of industrial countries be liberalized.

The Round of negotiations begun at Punta del Este creates the opportunity for this to be achieved. It is hoped that a broadening group of developing countries will be substantively engaged in all aspects of this negotiation. A good beginning has been made in this respect with the entry of Mexico and the decision of China to reenter GATT.

To ensure that the group able to avail itself of the opportunities available in trade is enlarged, it is important that the role of the World Bank and the IMF be recognized and supported. Only with adequate financing are many countries able to find the courage and organization needed to achieve the reforms necessary for an effective trading strategy.

A major contribution to the strengthening of the world economy would be made if the GATT Secretariat would be accorded more independent authority. If it can achieve a continuing role in interpreting agreed upon rules, in adjudicating disputes, and hopefully in annual monitoring and review of individual country trade policy developments, the prospects would be much brighter for a strengthened international trading system within which developing countries can effectively participate.

Comment

John Whalley

JOHN WHALLEY: I found the paper by David and Costas extremely interesting. I guess from my perspective I may be mis-summarizing it, and they will correct me no doubt if I am wrong, but the paper set out very clearly the flow of argument that one would very commonly hear in developed countries, certainly in North America and some in Europe, along the following lines: that growth and liberal trade regimes are clearly related.

So liberalization is good for developing countries. At an institutional level, there are a couple of institutions sitting out there. There is the GATT, and we know a little bit about the GATT. It is a framework for trying to achieve more liberalization. There is the IMF, which used to be concerned with fixed exchange rates between developed countries and with maintaining parities and trying to ensure convertibility in its very old days going back to the late 1940s and early 1950s.

But since 1973, it has gotten involved more with developing countries, and the developing countries themselves have come into the GATT system with special and differential status, including

Article XVIII(b) which really gives them carte blanche to use trade restrictions for balance-of-payments purposes as they like.

When this happened, it reflected what one might call an "old line" of thinking on development, that, in fact, a certain degree of protection for these countries was good because that would help them to industrialize and industrialization was equated with growth, and therefore protection made some sense.

This was the development thinking of the past. Things have changed and people don't really believe that in quite the same way.

Then if you look at the activities of the Bank and the Fund, they have been focusing very heavily on trade policy and trying to encourage countries to move along toward more liberal trading orders.

Some conditionality has been used, and that has been helpful in moving countries along the path towards liberalization. Now we face the Uruguay Round and what is happening in the Round? Well, there is a lot of heterogeneity among developing countries, but now there are again new opportunities for liberalization.

There have been a lot of developing countries that have come into this process in various ways. A number of them found themselves to be surprisingly important in Punta del Este in the ministerial meeting which launched the Round, and there are a lot of references in the declaration to developing countries. They have become active in the 14 negotiating groups, in the group negotiating goods, and they have made a lot of proposals.

So there are some opportunities there. There may be a possibility of some kind of deal that could involve perhaps some form of discipline in the Article XVIII(b) area, which is this balance-of-payments thing, in return for something in the safeguards area in the developed countries, which is one of their problems in Article XIX.

Now from the point of view of somebody coming from the developed world, and I say especially in my personal case having gone through a graduate program in North America, this seems so reasonable and so obvious and so straightforward. The first thing that we learn in basic trade courses is that for any small open-price-taking economy, free trade is the best policy, and it is all so straight-forward. What on earth is the problem?

I think as all of us know, if you get involved in discussions with people from Brazil and India, they will think that this is just crazy. I am putting it in those extreme terms because there is another intellectual argument which I think is at the heart of many of these debates.

Now just to give you my own background, I have been involved with a project for the Ford Foundation for the last couple of years. It is a project involving 11 developing countries. We have scholars in those countries who are in universities but involved or connected to the policy process in their countries. They have each been prepar-ing studies, but we have had a lot of meetings, and when we meet we finish up in long discussions on the trading system.

We meet with government people, and we have had tremendous support from the international agencies. Patrick, for the GATT Secre-tariat, has been to some of our meetings, but other people from the Secretariat, the Bank, UNCTAD, and so on also attend, and what has come to me from these discussions are these alternative views.

Through the filter of these individuals, the impression I have is that opinion within these countries are also extremely different, extremely heterogeneous. But what I suggest is that this alternative view does have an intellectual credibility, and it needs to be taken seriously. It is very different, and it is important. It leads one to discussions of the trading system.

Now before I launch into this, let me just give you the countries that I have been involved in to give you a sense of my background.

In Latin America we have Brazil, Mexico, Argentina, and we have Costa Rica as a small country. In Africa, we have Kenya, Tan-zania, and Nigeria; and in Asia, we have India, China, the Philip-pines, and South Korea. It is not necessarily that balanced a view, but it is a view as I see it.

The argument, I think, would go along the following lines and reflects many of the comments I made earlier. Let's begin with the

GATT and look at the system. The way I would characterize the system is as fundamentally mercantilist.

Economists often say that and then think that it shows how silly the system is. But I would suggest that it is not that way at all. You have to dig deeper and figure out why it is so mercantilist.

Under mercantilism, one views imports as inherently bad and exports as inherently good—as desirable. It is quite opposite to a traditional economic argument about the gains from trade, that there is no inherent difference between imports and exports. Some are viewed as good and some as bad. You just want to trade and maximize the gains from trade.

If you take that view, you always want to unilaterally liberalize. But, no, the system is really a system of arrangements trying to deal with domestic restrictions on trade in light of these mercantilist pressures.

Now what are these mercantilist pressures? Let me just give you an example. If you take a developed country democracy that has elections every four or five years, the politicians know that on any trade policy issue the people who take those issues very seriously are the export interests who can get access and the competing import interests who will suffer if anything happens to them. They will be vociferous in defending their interests.

The argument is that their views will come to dominate in the political process and in the outcome. The argument is that in a voting process, people vote every four or five years for a bundle of issues.

They don't vote on every single issue as it comes up. With bundled issues, the wider consumer interest will never be represented because individual consumers will vote on a whole range of other issues, including personality of the politicians and so on. But people who feel intensely about those matters will vote on the basis of those issues. The politicians are maximizing individuals, and if they are vote maximizing in choosing where they stand on a policy question, they have to trade off what is going on on the export side, where they can pick up some votes, and what is going on on the import side, where they can lose them.

You might say that the simple way to deal with all this is just to move to referenda, have a referendum on every little trade policy matter. The difficulty with that is that it totally undermines all notions of representative democracy. We would be sitting in front of our TV sets every night voting on all of these issues as they come up.

One of the essential features of the democratic process is delegation of authority with input by individuals into this process of government. So protection and, in this case, the democratic process are integrally linked.

The same kinds of pressures are there in developing countries, even if you are dealing with military-type regimes or fledgling democracies. So you begin from this starting point of the mercantilist structure, and what is going on then is optimizing behavior by politicians.

What the whole system is about then is politicians trading things back and forth between themselves, trying to get things which they regard as inherently desirable. The system is designed to facilitate liberalization of trade by allowing trade between politicians to take place.

There are two quite separate elements of the current GATT system. On the one hand, there is a set of principles to which the system aspires, and we often tend to concentrate on those to the exclusion of the other component. In the GATT system, the two pillars really are MFN, on the one hand, which says you can't discriminate between sources of supply up to a national border, and national treatment, on the other hand, which says you can't discriminate once you get beyond the national border.

But every economist that I have ever spoken to says, "Well, wait a minute, MFN is just inherently desirable because it prevents discrimination between suppliers. How could you possibly disagree with MFN?"

Well, in terms of traditional economic analysis, I don't think one can. But when you look at it in terms of what it does to the negotiating process, the problems appear. As a negotiating rule, it is clearly deficient. It is deficient in the sense that if you have large countries negotiating with small countries, large countries can't negotiate with small countries in an MFN system because if they give a small country anything in these mercantilist terms, that automatically is given to everybody else.

So even if the large countries are telling the small countries, "Come on into the system, come further into the system," there is, in fact, an impediment built right into the system which prevents the bargaining. As I say, that is in no way meant to reflect badly on the underlying principle.

If we keep following this line, you have to then examine where the system came from and how it got where it is. The way I see it, it is something which has evolved from the 1940s. It is a mechanism through which the developed countries deal with each other and exchange these concessions and deal with the competing interests that push those concessions.

In the immediate postwar years, there was a multilateralization of the prewar agreements. Of course, the U.S. case had been initiated in 1934 through the Reciprocal Trade Agreements Act. But there were a series of negotiations that went fairly quickly, there were some concessions and there was an issue of how substantial they were. They were mainly tariff bindings, and at this point Europe, in particular, was still in a regime of having substantial exchange controls.

But after 1957 or 1958, with the formation of the European Community, it accelerated rapidly, and the EC, United States, and to some extent, Japanese issues started being dealt with through this system. These countries got together and bargained their barriers down.

In addition, beyond the GATT there is a monetary component to the system. That is really the IMF component, and I see the Fund as central and integral to the system. I think if you look at the writings of Keynes between 1943 and 1945, it is very clear how he saw this whole system. The 1930s had been bedeviled not by a retaliatory trade war, through tariffs being erected back and forth between countries, but by competitive devaluations. This created a need for stability in the global financial system.

There had to be a fixed exchange rate regime. These had to be long-run parities which were defensible. So the Fund was to be the vehicle for achieving that, eventually achieving full convertibility, allowing for surpluses to be recycled from surplus countries to deficit countries to defend parities and then to move forward to real trade liberalization.

In other words, convertibility was a precondition of meaningful trade liberalization under the GATT. Financial matters and financial issues were separated from the GATT because of the need for this precondition. In the GATT there is an implicit contract to convertibility which precedes the explicit contract of reciprocal bargaining.

So that is the system, and the LDCs have come into the system. I think it is very important for us to see how and see why.

The developing countries are very different, both in terms of their size and their underlying economic structure. That creates problems for the system that I have just described when the developing countries arrive on the doorstep.

Pretty early on in the GATT, in the 1950s, it was noted that there was not much reciprocal bargaining going on involving the developing countries. If you look at the Haberler Report in 1958, it is very clear that lack was a driving force behind thinking about the developing countries, what should we do about them, how can we deal with their problems. Tariff escalation was one such problem.

A lot of the thinking at that time led to UNCTAD and the doctrines which are associated with Raul Prebisch around these years and were extraordinarily important. But entering the mid-1960s, there was a combination of factors which led to special treatment for developing countries.

The application of GATT disciplines to the developing countries which were in the system slowly became more and more lax. There were fewer consultations and so on.

There was a sense that the newly independent states which were emerging from a colonial past somehow should be encouraged and should be brought into this system and, maybe, treated in some special way.

People believed in the kind of developmental model that Costas was describing. And there was clearly a geopolitical interest. All of those things were there. So the developing countries came into the system with special and differential status, and the special and differential component is very clear.

It says that you are special in the sense that you don't need to liberalize, you don't need to take on any GATT obligations, you don't need to bargain, nonreciprocity, all of the things which now create so many problems. The differential component was really tied into the need for preferential access in developed country markets to offset the export pessimism which bedeviled these countries. People believed that they would never generate enough export earnings to deal with their balance-of-payments constraints.

So the developing countries then came into the system and, in a sense, there they have remained since those days. The Tokyo Round took place with no huge negotiations between developed and developing countries. Many issues impinged on them and there have been other developments outside of the system, as with the voluntary restraint agreements.

Now what we are doing is saying that we are very concerned about this situation. We want the developing countries to come further in, and it is a very different situation for South Korea as against India or Brazil. But when we are saying that we want them to come in, what we often neglect is the fact that there are barriers to their coming in further.

The barriers within the system are already down among the developed countries, so what is going to be reciprocally bargained? We are, in effect, now trying to bargain the new barriers we have created outside the system to try to force developing countries to lower their barriers in some way within the system.

The MFN problem is there in terms of a negotiating principle. We tell them, "Come on in," but how are we going to negotiate with them under an MFN system if they are all very small? Some of them, I know, are a little bit larger and there is some opportunity.

What to many of the developing countries are central interests from an international economic point of view, they regard as not being represented in the system. They are not on the agenda. For most of the countries in Africa, the main interest is commodities. That is not a barrier issue. It is, in terms of trade issues, an issue of stability; but it is their primary interest.

So when we look at the African countries and say they are all disinterested in the Uruguay Round, many of them would say, "Well, our interest is not reflected in the Round." There is a little bit in tariff escalation, but the central part is not there.

Then if you are dealing with the Latin American countries, they will say they are primarily concerned about the linkage between debt and trade issues. The reaction from the developed world is to say, "Well, that is not a negotiable interest. In the GATT, it is barrier-for-barrier, and we don't even know what it means to negotiate on debt." If debt is linked to trade in some way, such as firmer assurances that debt service will be prompt in return for removal of steel quotas to generate LDC exports, there may be agreement. But debt is the central interest for many of the developing countries.

Another important concern is that financial liberalization in developing countries is not being regarded as a negotiable concession because it is not really admissible to the kind of system that we have designed.

So this outcome has led to a development in the system which I guess I would loosely characterize along the following lines. First of all, there is a lack of discipline among developing countries in the system. They have really come into the system and not been forced to liberalize.

Martin Wolf has referred to developing countries as "noncontracting" contracting parties to the GATT. They come in with no obligations.

As a result, the developed countries can de facto break any rules they like whenever it is convenient to do so, and there are no formal sanctions on them in terms of withdrawal of concessions.

There are a lot of fights about the GATT regarding legality of certain things and whether the Multi-Fibre Arrangement (MFA) is a fundamental derivation of the GATT, which is what some of the developing countries say.

We have had a growth of textile agreements, voluntary restraint agreements, and so on, and there is no mechanism for the developing countries to restrain this growth of protection in the developed world.

The system has also created some weapons for the developing countries which cause endless frustration for the developed countries. Because the developed countries are so wedded to a multilateral system, GATT legality becomes a very important weapon. It is about the only weapon you have if you are a developing country.

They say, "Well, look, we came into the system. This is special and differential status. This is what it says and this is it." We get back to debates on is the MFA a derivation of the GATT, and we have these long discussions which are frustrating for both sides.

The system also creates the opportunity for developing countries to threaten to deny multilateral legitimacy to a negotiation as a way of forcing other items to be taken more seriously in agenda setting.

On the services issue, it seems to me that is exactly what happened. The Brazilian position was that, we can't deal with services, we have to deal with old issues. We have to deal with all of these broken promises, and their list would be the MFA and CAP and other things and so on.

The system has also divided the developing countries to some extent. What we have is a system in which many of the small countries have become far more concerned with preferences than they have with the multilateral system.

There are now some seventy countries in Lome. The CBI countries really think they have something, and it is part of the geopolitical interest of the more major parties. But in this Ford Foundation project, when I talk to our Kenyan participant, the view I get is that Kenya basically is not interested in the MTN.

They are very interested in Lome. That is a very major negotiation for them, and they are very interested in the preferential trade agreement in Africa, and they are interested in their coffee quota.

I say to them, "Well, what do you really want from the trading system?" They say, "Lome with the U.S." So the small countries have been pulled off into this system. You have a group of NICs for whom access has become very important, but they don't know how to proceed.

The Koreans have shown initially a large amount of potential interest in reciprocal bargaining. There was even talk a few years ago of possible formal acknowledgment of changes in S&D.

But they feel that as they have become more liberal and indicated these things, they have distanced themselves from other developing countries. Consequently, they have received more pressure from the developed countries than many other small developing countries who have larger barriers, and this has created major internal political problems in Korea. So the Koreans are searching for a role.

Should they just say, "Well, we should behave like a developed country, 35 percent of GNP is traded, 95 percent in manufactures; we have major barriers in the United States and Europe and so on, and we must focus on these access problems." Or, should they maneuver in a different way. They do not know where to go. It is not clear to them in the multilateral system as it now stands that their interest can be dealt with through reciprocal bargaining.

Then there are a few larger countries who don't have the preferences, who perhaps don't have the major access problems of the smaller Asian NICs, who have become very concerned about the whole system itself and very systemic in their behavior. Brazil and India are the two classic cases.

Brazil obviously has more access issues and more access concerns than India. They have a very different approach and a very different view of the world, but they are in a different group. The system to some extent has produced this.

On top of that, there is a frustration of developed countries that goes through a whole range of things with GSP graduation, threats of various actions, more tensions. If you look at the logic of the system, and if it is a mercantilist system, and if the problem is that you have given S&D to developing countries to go a certain way, the logic would say that you actually have to give them more to get them to go further. What is happening is that through the system, there are attempts to take away from a developing country things which have already been given.

Once again, they resort to challenging GATT legality and the integrity of the system.

So that is how I see the system as having developed. Where does this leave me or where does this lead the discussions that I have had with many of these people? I guess the system has delivered on the developed-to-developed-country liberalization. It has harnessed the mercantilist pressures in countries of comparable size and economic structure to allow for bargaining between politicians and to use that external bargaining to put some discipline on domestic political interests.

It has not delivered as regards developed-to-developing-country situations. It has, in fact, made the situation worse because of barrier asymmetry. The extent to which barriers have come down between developed countries is now making bargaining between developed and developing countries even more difficult.

Issues of central importance to developing countries are not in the system, nor is there any simple way for them to be injected into the system.

There is a clash between MFN on the one hand and S&D on the other hand. So I guess where I finish up is that the problem is not really the countries and the participants in the system and the sets of tensions which exist between certain developing countries and developed countries.

The problem is the system itself. It is a system which generates these difficulties. We need to understand that to begin to discuss the problem. That doesn't mean to say that there is an overwhelmingly attractive alternative to this current system but I think once we begin to understand that, the discussion becomes a little bit easier.

Now what to do about all this? I begin from the position that there is no well developed theory of bargaining. Nobody really knows how bargaining should proceed.

We have a situation here where we basically have constrained bargaining. We put all these rules down in the system and then say, "Let's have some bargains and they have to be multilateral and they have to conform to this rule and that rule." It is very different from labor negotiations where nobody ever puts any constraints in the bargain before it takes place.

We think we all know why. We do not like groups of countries going off and negotiating things between themselves and messing up the system to the disadvantage of other countries. But with no theory, it is very hard to make a prior argument that one particular approach is going to dominate another. So I think we are going to have to be creative in dealing with this.

It is also very difficult for me to see how one breaks out of the current system in any huge way. Countries have undertaken GATT obligations. Those are obligations that they take very seriously. You are not going to suddenly unwind all of these obligations.

The injection of new issues into reciprocal bargaining is very hard. But one implication may be that we should, perhaps, worry a little less about the system itself than we have done in recent years.

There is an element in the thinking in many countries in which the system itself has become the object of policy. The objective of policy is to maintain and strengthen the multilateral system.

What we are neglecting is that the system is a means toward an end. The end is to achieve liberalized trade. The system is a means to that end. Protecting, strengthening, and focusing on the system may divert us from that objective.

For instance, there are currently U.S.–Mexico bilaterals going on. Well, one might say there is some reciprocal bargaining going on that can take place because it is outside the formalized system, and that is good. You may be concerned about the MFN implications of that.

But if the objective is just to liberalize trade, perhaps we should focus on methods of liberalization rather than the system. Also, I would argue that the system itself tends to be what I call "creative" in fostering various liberalization opportunities.

Where politicians have things to trade, they should be able in the final analysis to find ways to do that trade. If we have so many impediments built into the system, maybe that is telling us something. We have had such little trade between developed and developing country politicians that we have to find ways for that to take place.

The U.S.–Canada agreement, as I see it, is a partial rejection by the Canadians of the multilateral process as a way of securing its economic interest.

Finally, developed countries might also need to think quite creatively. One thing to think about, which was implicit in Bob's paper, is a need to recognize that they have to have something more concrete to offer to developing countries in a mercantilist setting. If barriers have come down, what developing countries really want is bindings on those barriers.

They have formal bindings in a GATT sense, but there are no bindings in terms of the voluntary restraint system. If there is firmer discipline on those voluntary restraint agreements, maybe there is some way we can move forward to some bargaining and there are some opportunities to bargain.

Let me wrap up with three final comments. One is that we have not mentioned any macro issues in all of this. There are certain things going on outside the system which I think are also very important.

We are getting a lot of tensions currently in the system as we are moving forward to this Round. The higher we can get OECD growth rates the more we relieve tensions from the mercantilist point of view. With growth, export interest gets some access and the pressures from export interests abroad trying to come into import markets are relieved. So to some extent looking outside the system may help us a little bit.

There are also some major macro issues I think for developing countries. If you take say the U.S. trade deficit and you look at this huge growth in imports from developing countries that was mentioned earlier as that trade deficit really begins to unwind, and if indeed there is a major servicing problem because of U.S. foreign debt out until the 1990s, it may well be that the trade prospects for developing countries are changed more dramatically by that than anything in fact which goes on in the Uruguay Round.

My second comment is about the Round itself. I think we have touched on that in our discussions a little bit, but there is a mixture of optimism and pessimism which pervades the air. It might just be worth injecting that a little bit into the discussion.

The optimism seems to be because lots of countries came into the Punta del Este process. They have taken it further. They are on the negotiating committees. We have perhaps 140 proposals. So there is a lot of activity and they are in the Round.

The pessimism is that these Rounds are usually dominated by U.S.–EC and discussions and debates and eventually resolutions with the Japanese, and that to some extent agriculture is the key to this one. Agriculture is extraordinarily difficult for various reasons we could go into later. In turn, U.S.–EC tensions seem to be being elevated with the fall in the dollar.

They have a trade bill which is pending. It is a presidential election year. We have weakened U.S. hegemony and one could go on and on down the list, and I hear a lot of people who are fairly cautious about the Uruguay Round.

Finally, views I have picked up from discussions with people from these various countries, people here may have some interest in. Perhaps I will just run down a few of them quickly. I mentioned Kenya which is very pragmatic, no interest in the system.

Next we have Tanzania. The Tanzanian interest is very, very different. Their major interest is commodities. They are also very systemic, G-77, UNCTAD, and so on, and there really seems to be a divorce between their official diplomatic posture and their narrow economic interest which they do not really seem to pursue in any concrete way in terms of the trading system. Instead, they seem to recognize that their major problems are domestic policy problems and that is the focus of the trade discussion. That is kind of overwhelming to them.

Nigeria is another country where there is almost no participation in the Uruguay Round. In Nigeria, 99 percent of exports currently are in oil. There really are no major access issues they have currently. There are some potential issues in agriculture, maybe even some small scale manufacturing.

In the case of Asia, in the Chinese case what we pick up is a lot of concern over GATT membership, but it is not quite clear why they want to be in the GATT or what they expect to obtain from the GATT. They have a major focus on textiles and textile quotas.

The Indian case I have already hinted at. Of all the countries in the group we are talking to, it is the one which takes the most extreme line. Also, in terms of the intellectual climate within countries it is extraordinarily sensitive.

There is a tie-in in the Indian case, I think, between broader foreign policy objectives and their trade policies stance. This even goes so far as an argument that if you receive foreign aid from developed countries, the threat of cessation of the aid will be used against you to change your foreign policy stance. And that may even stretch to certain components of trade, so you have to be very cautious in your dealing with developed countries.

Discussion

DR. LOW: Professor Whalley seems to be arguing that there is a need to look for more imaginative approaches to trade issues and not be so concerned with the system, since the system after all is a means to an end. The downside risks of that sort of approach need to be questioned. What happens, in particular, when the pressures are for protection and not for liberalization? Will the system be able to provide any kind of support to counterbalance protectionist forces if it has been weakened as a result of some compromise or other made to secure trade liberalization in the short term?

As regards the paper by Dr. Finch and Dr. Michalopoulos, there is reference to the possibility of developing countries acquiring credit for liberalization which they have undertaken in the past unilaterally. It is not entirely clear how this would work in practice. In the case of tariffs, negotiating currency would only be secured through bindings, and not as a result of a unilateral, unbound tariff reduction. Similarly, a developing country removing or reducing quantitative restrictions would probably be considered to have disinvoked or partially disinvoked Article XVIII. So once again the question of negotiation credit would not arise. This is not to say that there would never be circumstances where past actions could be put on the negotiating table, but there is a need for greater specificity on this point.

DR. PREEG: I would like to make a couple of comments based on the number of provocative things said. Let me start by saying that I had the pleasure and the distinction, along with David and one or two others here, to be at Punta for the ministerial meeting, and there was a brief period of euphoria there.

Everybody was very pleased, everybody except perhaps one person I should say, when it was moved that this be called the Uruguay Round, because this showed that developing countries were going to be much more important in this GATT Round. The one unhappy person, incidentally was rumored to be the mayor of Punta del Este because, in keeping with the Tokyo Round, he wanted the new Round to be the Punta del Este Round, with implications for tourism in Punta, but that is a footnote to history.

In any event, the euphoria obviously has dissipated. We can now see very difficult issues of S&D and the role of the developing countries in the GATT, particularly the more advanced developing countries. They will arise in agriculture and in various other parts of the negotiation. Perhaps a better name would have been the Article XVIII/XIX Round, but then only the cognoscenti of GATT nomenclature would know what we were talking about. In any event, that would be an optimistic title, to predict such a package deal possible.

One of my problems, having heard today how critical and elusive these fundamental issues of balance of payments and commitments by the more advanced developing countries are—and it is a particular problem as chief economist in A.I.D.—is that I don't know what a developing country is.

I have looked into the GATT and I don't see a definition anywhere, or anything in its history as to what is a developing country. Until the Tokyo Round, this wasn't too much of an issue because developing countries were a relatively nonthreatening group of non-communist, non-OECD countries. We have been looking at and updating the criteria lately, however, to try to define more clearly, a developing country in commercial terms. We have looked at the so-called Gang of Four in particular. Taiwan, of course, is not a GATT participant, and Hong Kong is a city that is going from a colony to a part of a bigger country, and it maintains free trade anyhow. But two of them, Korea and Singapore, are countries and Uruguay Round participants. We tested a number of criteria related to the level of development, not just per capita income but other measures as well, and particularly trade competitiveness in manufactures, which is where GATT reciprocal commitments are concentrated. And for all criteria tested, these two countries received high marks. They measured comparably with Ireland, Greece, and Spain, as lower tier OECD countries. We also compared Korea and Singapore in 1985, with Italy and Japan in 1965, when those countries had already long been full GATT participants, and Korea and Singapore showed up reasonably well.

These are only two countries, but what do you do about them? Are they or aren't they industrialized countries? Obviously, they can claim eligibility as developing countries, for example, under Article XVIII(b), not that Korea or Singapore has a particular balance-of-payments problem, but who decides whether it is justified or not? What if we said, "We now consider them industrialized countries by any measure and if they have counterarguments, we are willing to listen?" I believe the whole graduation question is coming to the fore as these top echelon countries of what used to be the LDC grouping are less and less clearly defined or not defined at all. Indeed, I believe graduation is going to come much more to the fore during the course of the GATT Round.

Moreover, it is not GSP especially that is of interest for this advanced group. They don't have that much benefit left with the restrictions put on them. It is on the other side, the questions of Article XVIII and reciprocity. We haven't talked much about the reciprocity issue today, and how we are going to deal with it in the GATT Round. I don't have a full answer with respect to reciprocity.

John Whalley asked what happens if developing countries decide to graduate, and I ask what happens if somebody else decides they are graduated? I would be happy to be enlightened on the GATT legal standing on these questions.

A more basic question of reciprocity arises when you have an asymmetric situation of, say Korea, with very high tariffs and widespread NTBs. We, in contrast, have relatively little to offer beyond liberalization of textile quotas. Reciprocity in these circumstances is an unclear concept. I recall at least three possible definitions. One is a neutral balance of trade impact in which each side reduces barriers enough so that increased exports and imports balance out.

The second is a linear, or equal percentage, reduction which was the basis for Kennedy Round tariff cuts. It is also discussed for troop and missile reductions. It amounts to going a certain percentage of the way to zero. The ultimate objective, of course, would be if everyone goes to zero, which is the basis for U.S. agricultural proposals in the Uruguay Round.

The third possible definition, which the European Community pursued in the Kennedy Round, is harmonization of protection at target levels. Higher tariffs are, by their nature, considered more onerous, so you have to bring down the high rates to a modest level before considering reductions in the lower levels. In some ways, perhaps the old EC formula could fit our relationship with the East Asians over the next few years.

Consistency, as we all know, is the hobgoblin of small minds. Reciprocity is not that cut and dried by any means, and I throw these thoughts out because I think we are evolving a very different trade relationship with developing countries that has been touched on around the table today. I think that over the next two or three years, we will have to come to grips with it more fully and explicitly.

DR. BALDWIN: I would like to talk a little bit about a couple of the points that John raised. First, the problem of small countries and large countries negotiating. Do I understand that what you are saying is that the multilateral approach cannot be used when you are negotiating between small countries and large countries?

I would like you to elaborate on why. I think I know the argument. Retaliation doesn't mean anything when a small country retaliates against a large country like the United States; the United States will just shift its exports to other countries. But what basically is the problem with the multilateral approach in dealings between small and large countries?

Does it finally come down to something about elasticities of supply, that if you reduce the same percent, you might be swamped in the small developing countries? Is that what you have in mind? If that is true, does it mean that lower percentage cuts by small countries are necessary to achieve reciprocity with large countries?

It seems to me that you are getting at a very basic problem. You are almost saying that multilateral negotiations can't work in small versus large country contexts and that bilateral negotiations are the useful approach.

I think in cases like U.S.–Canada and U.S.–Mexico, it is clear the United States is making concessions, not just on economic terms but for political and military reasons, and I think we are prepared to give up a lot economically to further these other objectives.

MR. KAUFFMAN: In the paper the speakers mentioned the need to move forward to strengthen the GATT Secretariat. I could imagine from the way they were talking a very large IMF/World Bank type of institution, with all kinds of teams roaming around the 100-some countries, that ends up contracting to do investigations of alleged violations of one rule or another. I just think a little more consideration of this might be useful; what really would be necessary, how would it be financed, would you put a tax on trade in order to pay for this?

The other institutions in some sense at least tend to be self-financing by now. I don't quite see how the GATT would be without something of that sort, so I wondered what other opinion might be about the nature and need for the expanded Secretariat?

DR. CONYBEARE: I have two comments. One is a question and one is a comment on one of John Whalley's remarks. With regard to a point made in the paper concerning the possibility of different types of coalition behavior in GATT, it made the quite interesting point that since the distinction between the developing and the developed countries isn't very meaningful any more, we should expect to see coalitions cutting across this traditional distinction.

But the only one you mentioned was the Cairns Group, and I was wondering whether you could give me examples of other possible coalitions. I would be interested to see what they might be.

My other remark was a comment on John Whalley's point about MFN being a barrier to negotiations because it creates public good problems. I think that is more of an analytic than a practical problem, because in practice, we get around that. We privatize the public good through principal supplier tactics, exchange controls, dual exchange rates, quotas, and things like that.

My recollection from the work of Mike Finger on GATT negotiations is that the United States has always used the principal supplier method of negotiation, even right up into the late 1960s, the Kennedy Round; so the MFN public good problem, I think, is more of an intellectual, analytic problem than a practical one, and I was wondering if you had any comment on that.

DR. KRUEGER: I am just going to briefly interject, because Mike carried his analysis up to date, or up to five years ago, and found that if the principal supplier method is employed in negotiations, very little of developing countries' exports would be excluded from application of MFN; they could capture most benefits of MFN by the principal supplier rule. This was a surprising finding, and goes along the lines that you are suggesting.

DR. MORSS: A couple of points. A number of the speakers have mentioned that things seem much more difficult today than they were at earlier negotiating sessions. This is because the threat of unemployment hangs over these sessions.

The other point I would make has to do with multilateral versus bilateral negotiations. As many of you know, the U.S. Treasury negotiates bilateral tax treaties with countries around the world, and I never stopped to think about whether this shouldn't be negotiated multilaterally. There is a whole set of corporate income tax base issues that in some sense require a global focus, but these have been negotiated bilaterally.

The attraction to me of the bilateral approach is that if the United States is sure that free trade is right, it can threaten to limit access to its markets. It certainly has been using that threat vis-à-vis Japan and is probably about to use it vis-à-vis Korea for better or worse.

DR. KRUEGER: All right. There were a couple of questions for John, too, so I will give our principal paper givers some time to respond to what they wish to and then John, I will give you a couple of minutes at the end to respond. David or Costas, who wants to start off?

DR. MICHALOPOULOS: I would like to elaborate on a couple of questions that were raised. First let me start with the credit idea. I think that what we were talking about there is fairly concrete. A number of developing countries have undertaken a significant amount of liberalization already, notwithstanding their commitment to the system that has permitted them to have special and differential and hence protected regimes. The point here is that they have done so outside of the GATT without any bindings.

As part of the process of negotiation, one could visualize a situation, where they would offer to simply bind what they have already liberalized and receive some credit for that. I don't think that they will get much credit if they were not to bind what they have already liberalized. But it would be advantageous for them to bind, if in fact they have decided to reduce their barriers. The only thing they would need to do more is to commit themselves not to increase barriers subsequently except in the GATT context.

John mentioned a lot about the question of the system and how the developing countries are committed to a system which permits them to carry on a number of protective policies; he mentioned Tanzania in this context. I find this very interesting because I think what is happening here is that the developing countries are frequently speaking with two voices. They speak with one voice in the GATT and with a different voice in the context of the conduct of their own trade policies, and the two sometimes reflect different perspectives about what their policies should be: on the one hand, from the standpoint of the foreign affairs officers, who typically represent developing countries in the GATT; and, on the other, from the standpoint of ministers of the economy, who take the actual decisions on specific trade policies in developing countries. The foreign affairs officers typically adopt the traditional protectionist line; ministers of the economy take a more pragmatic, less protectionist line.

There was another question about the nature of coalitions. The other coalition that we had in mind actually came up this morning and was a possible coalition in the question of safeguards on the matter of selectivity. I think one could visualize developing countries coalescing with some industrial countries opposing selectivity in safeguards.

Similarly, I could visualize some coalition between developing countries and Japan on issues related to voluntary export restraints. Japan, as you know, has been subjected to some of these restraints itself.

Then the other question was why are things more difficult in these negotiations. My sense of it is that it is probably easier to negotiate formula cuts or to develop mechanisms of negotiation on specific tariff-related measures when you are trying to reduce tariffs than when you are trying to negotiate nontariff measures. If, in fact, tariff negotiations are going to be less important in this Round than negotiations on nontariff measures or general rules, I feel that such negotiations could pose more difficulties in the participation of the developing countries.

DR. FINCH: The thing that I would like to stress is that we were trying to develop the broader connection between institutions and development. Although politicians have a role, certainly the financial institutions are interested in results. Therefore, we have to weigh in on the side of actions which are likely to promote needed growth. The lending agencies are going to be on the side of liberalization.

On the more political level, I suppose being an Australian here, you are not that confident that multilateralism is always fair. It seems that the thought that somehow in the early stage perhaps you are sort of up for bids between clashing coalitions, and it may be that you can get a reasonably good deal in the first negotiation, but if you end up with clear regional spheres of influence, that is not exactly the way that I think most developing countries should want to go, and they should be very much aware of the downside risk of going that route.

Even for Canada, the thought that it was going to submerge the culture is not something negligible, and there is a much better protection against some of these political things if you are dealing in a broad group.

That is not to say that he isn't quite right, of course, that the situation is very difficult even within a multilateral group. It is just that you must be trying to develop techniques of working within that if you are going to get the best protection.

I think that you throw up your hands particularly at this stage where quite clearly the main thrust of world development is toward regionalism, and there is a very clear readiness in exchange rate matters, trade matters, and in capital to be thinking that the United States will look after Latin America, Europe will look after Africa, and Japan will look after East Asia, and that is not a comfortable environment for the developing countries to think about.

It is just like some of the forces in Canada where there is a sort of fear that it was best to get out and confront the issues in negotiation, and I think that in the world in general, the developing countries should start to fear a little that they are going to lose again to this regionalism if they don't try to get out and organize.

I suppose the cost of getting into teams, the GATT has a Secretariat of what, 300 people at present?

DR. LOW: Three hundred and twenty roughly, I think.

DR. FINCH: The Fund has 1,500 or 1,600; roughly quintupling the size of GATT. When we were trying to improve the consultations process we approached GATT and the Fund—I am still using the past tense—but the GATT sort of said they didn't have enough people to even give you the state of say German restrictions or what has been happening there.

I think there must be a limited number which could be added which could start to put some life into having GATT more than a passive Secretariat and in the position of being able to be authoritative on what is happening in the area.

Yes, it adds a little to the cost, maybe Japan or someone will fund it.

[Laughter.]

DR. FINCH: But these things certainly would be beneficial to have an improved strength in that regard.

DR. WHALLEY: Again, the issue was raised of bilateralism versus multilateralism and let me just say this. In my remarks I think I said that I didn't think there was any natural way to go, and it seems to me that there is a big difference between the two.

With the bilateral approach, it does seem to me that pairs of countries can negotiate more quickly. It is easier for them to trade concessions from a reciprocal bargaining point of view. The reason we don't like that is that the outcome may not be desirable from the point of view of other countries.

So what the multilateral system does is place rules on any negotiations that countries could enter into in terms of the outcome. There is a trade-off between the rules on the one hand, and you may want those rules, and the speed of negotiation those rules permit. I think Patrick's point is very well taken.

If the developing countries are more concerned about the potential increase in barriers which they face, and they want to have basically an insurance policy over those rules, the multilateral system may well offer them much more.

On the other hand, if the objective is to have speedy negotiation, I think you can argue that there are impediments in the multilateral system, and that makes the bilateral route more attractive.

One other comment on bilateral issues is from a U.S. point of view. It has always struck me as very strange that the United States should be so wedded to the multilateral system because if you only have an economic interest, it doesn't make sense for a large country to negotiate with a series of smaller countries in a multilateral system; everything is always extended through MFN and, in fact, from a negotiation point of view, you would have more power and more control and more influence with bilateral negotiations.

So the conclusion that I come to is that presumably the U.S. interest is intertwined with its geopolitical interest.

From the point of view of smaller countries, they want multilateral systems because they want the rules and security of a multilateral set of arrangements around any forms of negotiations they have with a large country. They want to prevent the large country from picking them off one by one.

So we always say to the developing countries, come into the multilateral system because we get the benefits of no discrimination and all the rest of it, so there are all sorts or elements of paradox here which make it possible. I think it is very difficult to say a priori which is better; but the outcome from the system that we now confront, it seems to me causes us to think about it.

Finally, Bob raised the issue of MFN and the barrier to liberalization. What I had in mind I think John very accurately summarized. It is simply that if you have an MFN system where any bilateral concessions are extended to everybody else, when a large country negotiates with a small country and gives a small country something, that concession is given to everybody. So large countries have relatively limited incentives to negotiate with the small countries from a mercantilist point of view. I was grateful to both John and Anne for raising the issue of practicality, and I must look at some of that literature.

DR. KRUEGER: What we need to focus on most is discerning the possibilities for action and the policies that could be undertaken that might make some difference to the outcome of the new Round. I thought I might just kick off by addressing some of the issues that have been raised and a couple that haven't been raised that may be of some importance in all of this.

First, Gale Johnson's paper focused, to some extent, on the role of knowledge and information underpinning the gains to be had from the liberalization system and/or the losses that would be incurred by further bifurcation and bilateralization, or for that matter, movements toward autocracy.

That is obviously an important issue and there are obviously some things to be done with that. Related to that, and something that I learned today, is the threat on the supply management side on agriculture; one important set of policy issues may relate to how that kind of a threat can be headed off.

The second issue which Ed Schuh raised was the whole link between exchange rates, trade, debt, and other issues. One question that comes up over and over is that there is, after all, within many of the OECD governments, a concern over developed country growth. There is another concern over developing countries' indebtedness, and there is another set of concerns over trade issues.

Somehow or other, the institutional arrangements within countries are not such as to harness the mutuality of interest which exists internationally. Instead, one sees some degree of self-defeating policies resulting from the disparate positions advanced within governments; by finance ministers who are typically more free trade oriented in their fora, agricultural ministers responding to other interests in their own arena, and trade ministers inevitably responding to protectionist interests in their fora. It seems to me that at least some questions need to be addressed regarding how one might somehow try more systematically or institutionally to address these domestic incompatibilities, and get the interests that are more on the side of opening up the country's trade regime (i.e., those most responsible for the developing country's debt and so on) more closely aligned with other domestic interests on the side of getting an appropriate bargain in the multilateral trading system.

An issue that didn't come up is that it was very important earlier on that the United States take some leadership in focusing on the system. John had some comments earlier as to why a large country might have an interest in the system. I would argue that the large country has to have an interest in the system in a way that the small country does not. It is from this perspective that I perceive a failure of U.S. leadership; failing to continue to espouse free trade, and taking a position in terms of its parochial interest as if it were a small country.

Furthermore, the perception that the United States no longer occupies a leadership position in matters of international trade—a perception that seems to afflict a growing number of American policymakers—is, I submit, (a) wrong, and (b) debilitating to the international economy.

It seems to me that policy proposals of any kind, and our A.I.D. sponsors here are perhaps in a better position than some of us to say how one does this, require that the American position be somewhat cleaner on the trade issue. It seems to me that this is one very important step that could be taken to improve prospects.

Are we still committed to an open multilateral system as contrasted with a multipolar world where you might have a trading block organized around East Asia, another trading block organized around North America, and another organized around Europe?

I have no doubt but that the United States has a strong systemic interest in a multilateral system. Certainly from the viewpoint of small countries, I can even conceive of a situation or many situations where the system itself may protect politicians from the pressures which otherwise arise from their own particular and special interests.

This is something that really hasn't come out very much today. That is, if you build a system where the poor politician is sitting there on the firing line and everybody in the district is going to go to him because they want protection for shoes and carpets and wallpaper and what have you, that is a system which inevitably, in some sense, will have more difficulty than a system in which it is not perceived that the politician is the first line of defense.

It seems to me on that score, there might even be some scope for educating politicians that it is not always in their self-interest to be right in the middle of some of these trade policy issues.

Suppose we decided today that after some deep and serious thinking we thought there was an institution that in some sense could better fulfill all these good multilateral purposes than GATT. The question is, could you get there or are you better off anyway to stay with GATT and see what we can do to strengthen it?

I guess I would take the viewpoint that we have had so much difficulty in terms of even keeping the international institutions going that to try to open it up at this stage and start from scratch would yield a Pandora's box. It is much better to look and see what you can do within the system to maintain a commitment to open trading and binding treaties. I would be very reluctant to see us coming up with proposals which in any sense undercut GATT.

It seems to me that we need to address what proposals are possible, what is it that might have a shot at success in terms of bargains. The things I come out of today with are several.

First, there are different groups of developing countries and developed countries with different interests. If you bargain on an item-by-item basis, you will never pull all those interests together.

If there is going to be a meaningful global vision, if that is the right word, and a leap forward instead of something very small, it strikes me that there is going to have to be a way around the problem John Whalley mentioned: you can't expect to have 90 countries sitting around and doing their one-on-one kind of thing and then put it together.

Some other form of packaging is going to be desirable. One can imagine groups of countries—the agricultural exporters (the Cairns Group perhaps being one) or some of the other groups of interest— that might cut across developing–developed differences.

It might be that negotiations over different tariff cutting formulae are desirable where, for example, developed countries might go with the full cut; NICs might have an intermediate position, perhaps reducing 70 percent now and the remaining 30 percent over ten years; middle-income countries, like Brazil, might reduce 30 percent now and 70 percent over the next ten years; and, then, low-income countries which might never be expected to reduce barriers more than 30 percent.

One can think of formulae like this. Part of the problem right now is that there is no mechanism doing this, and that raises all the problems that John discussed. What about different sectors? Should these be addressed differently?

It seems apparent that unless the sectoral interests can somehow be combined so that it isn't all agriculture on agriculture and manufactures on manufacturing, there are going to continue to be some of these problems. The same thing applies to different issues, somehow or another we can't take each one by itself and hope to get very far.

Somehow or another it seems to me that what cries out from all this discussion, is the need for some kind of creative bundling of these issues. Bob Baldwin had the S&D versus the CVD and the antidumping code.

There is the issue of the Multi-Fibre Arrangement, and there you don't have two interests. You have more. You have the interests of the countries that currently have the quotas and that really wouldn't like too much to give them up. You have the new entrants who presumably have a greater interest in giving it up and, of course, you have the developed countries which will be in much better positions to relax MFA if at the same time some of the more advanced newly industrializing countries open up their markets.

How can this in some sense be bundled? What can we suggest beyond the old, "well, we will just wait and see what happens?" I have no idea how it should be done, but it seems to me it might be worth a little bit of our time thinking along these lines.

MR. VENEZIA: I work for an operating office and I was taken with the thought that the system that we have been hearing about today might be swamped by the U.S. trade deficit correction that is coming, and it was mentioned in passing as if it was a remote possibility.

But everything that one reads these days in the doom and gloom literature indicates that it *is* coming, and it is coming very fast. Listening today to what we were doing with the GATT reminds me of a meeting several years ago talking about the LA debt situation, which everybody saw coming very clearly and simply assumed that it would take care of itself, and indeed, I believe the LA debt situation overwhelmed or swamped the system.

If we make some pessimistic projections along these lines I think we can assume the following things. One, that the trade picture will change dramatically in the next five years; two, that the United States will, and you can almost say must, come into a balanced position on its trade; and three, that there will be major dislocations taking place within the LDCs.

Under these circumstances, I, sitting down in the engine room, ask those of you up on the bridge the following questions that I think A.I.D. has to address to remain relevant to trade and investment issues.

First, who will be our clients? They may not be the same that we have under our basic human needs rationale. There it is quite clear who our clients are, i.e., the LDCs. Under trade and investment, our clients can either be those U.S. interests that form the U.S. foreign assistance establishment, or the interests of the developing countries; but we will have to make choices.

The second is how will A.I.D. relate to the upcoming balance-of-payments correction dislocations? Will we pick up the pieces, which I would say is a reactive approach? Will we plan for the aftermath, which I would say tries to anticipate it? Do we assist in filling in the gaps that are created by the dollar flows that are going to be happening, which would be something that we would do during the process, or will we retreat to our ongoing basic human needs strategy saying it is just too big for A.I.D. to handle? Will we just walk away from it?

The next question I think we have to ask is what share of A.I.D. resources should we devote to these efforts if we get involved and how do we justify that to Congress, whatever share it is? The final question is how do we, A.I.D., fit within the overall U.S. government's effort to redress our trade imbalances?

In a funny way this is the opposite of the Marshall Plan which created us. We recycled dollars in those days. I don't know how to describe what we are going to be doing in the next ten years.

One additional question that occurs concerns conditionality. I think somebody mentioned it. Will we find ourselves putting conditionality on A.I.D. flows versus trade access? I don't know. Within the Asian and Near East Bureau, we are terribly interested in these trade and investment issues and we want to pursue them. We are asking ourselves what tools do we have as an agency to work in this area.

That is the agenda that I think is facing the agency in the next five years.

DR. WHALLEY: It seems to me the way things seem to be emerging—particularly multilaterally, and bilaterally to some extent—represents a change in the system yet again from another kind of perspective.

If you look at the way the GATT used to work in the early 1950s, during the first few Rounds, the GATT was a kind of cozy club. There were 20 some countries that would show up. The Rounds would last three months; they knew each other and were very friendly. The approach was coming along with things that they were willing to exchange from a mercantilistic point of view, and the bargain took place.

Now what seems to be happening, and I will use agriculture as an example, is that countries are identifying their interest. The U.S. and the Cairns Group identified agriculture as an interest.

The system is there, the component of the system, the GATT, the multilateral system, and the tactic seems to be to load up the pressure to force this accommodation. We want liberalization in Europe. We will get the Cairns Group, consolidate that with the U.S. and force, without coming into this arrangement in the old kind of way of saying, "Well, look, we want to do a deal, we think this and we have this."

In other words, it is as if participation is not proceeding with parties to these arrangements coming in with a deal they want to offer. They are coming in with a demand and hoping that if the pressure is enough, that somehow things will cave in.

Now what that suggests to me is that there are ways of moving forward constructively within the system; let me just give you some examples. It may well be on the kind of ad hoc piece-by-piece basis that one can carve out various kinds of changes which might be agreeable to parties that at the moment are not particularly contentious; the changes would have tremendous advantages in preventing future problems.

This is a rather obvious one bilaterally, but if you can use a bilateral negotiation to prevent an interest from being established, you can prevent problems later on. One of the concerns the Brazilians have is that five to ten years from now the Portuguese could be growing large amounts of coffee. It may seem crazy to us—coffee coming into CAP. But suppose that the Brazilians approach the Europeans and say, "Look, we are really concerned about this," (and the Kenyans, too). "We would like you to undertake some kind of binding." It would be just a simple binding on the crops that are in that program. I haven't heard anybody talk about this kind of a deal.

The problem at the moment is measurement of all these things and PSEs, and we can't agree what they are. That is a very simple idea, and it may be that the Brazilians and the Kenyans are willing to give a little bit for that.

Multilaterally, I think that financial liberalization is a major issue. It does seem to me that it is something that the developed countries could offer the developing countries which hopefully is constructive. It would involve the conversion of the existing implicit barriers and foreign exchange rationing into visible barriers in return for a commitment to convertibility.

If you take the premium value on rationed foreign exchange of 30 percent, in some country the deal would be: we will allow you to increase your tariff even if it is a bound tariff. We will let you increase that by 30 percent. This would appear very strange to the negotiating community because they would actually be increasing barriers in order to liberalize trade.

But increase that barrier and commit yourself to convertibility. If you deviate from convertibility, we are going to possibly look at various penalties on you. That is the deal, and it is moving down the GATT track of trying to get to some transparency and eventual negotiability. It is establishing those preconditions which were there on the developed countries. These are kinds of incremental changes. If you identify them from the point of view of not building pressure but just seeing what is feasible and what can be exchanged that may be constructive.

DR. MICHALOPOULOS: I want to come back to the issues of what this might mean for A.I.D. I think that one point that has been made about the international economy is that whenever there is an upheaval in the international economy, it is extremely important that developing countries have the kinds of flexibility of economic policies which would permit them to react to whatever international upheaval might be in store for them.

If one looks at the experience, countries which have tended to have more open economies surprisingly seem to have been able to weather shocks of various kinds better than countries which have had very inward looking policies and that sort of goes through most of the 1970s.

But if you have any changes in the international environment which you think would require adjustment on the part of the developing countries, it is very important that they have trade and foreign exchange policies which permit them to adapt quickly, so that what that means is that A.I.D. could be supportive of trade policies in the developing countries which permit them to develop this flexibility, this responsiveness, this openness to the international environment so as to permit them to adjust more readily to whatever international shocks you are visualizing. That is one point.

The second part of it is that the kind of things that A.I.D. has been able to do in the past has been to focus on institution building of various kinds. My own exposure to developing countries' trade ministries and trade institutions has been one that suggests that they need a lot of help from lots of sources, both to appreciate what is in the country's interest, to formulate policy, to persuade people in their environments about the importance of policies, and so forth.

I think A.I.D. can focus in that direction, but I also recognize that the capacity of A.I.D. to do so in the short term will be very limited; because the agency does not have the cadre and personnel who have been trained in that area, it would require work with consultants and other people who have the capability to provide this kind of assistance. Those are the two suggestions which are more concrete.

DR. SCHUH: I want to complement his comments. It has to do with extending it not only to the institutional development, which gives you a more flexible capacity (response capacity), but to training and education and the things that you do to the agricultural sector that give your economy more flexibility. So in many respects what you do to put yourself in a position to respond more flexibly to the trade shocks is nothing more than what you ought to be doing in any case.

I am struck by the rice diversification issue in Asia now where we are discovering that to get diversified out of rice, you have to make some significant changes in the infrastructure. You have the research capability to build, et cetera, but behind all that you still have this problem of formal schooling for rural population, training programs, et cetera.

DR. BALDWIN: I first want to comment on one of the points that John raised about the large country and what its interests are. He gave the answer, but I think it deserves some emphasis. Why doesn't the large country exploit its monopoly on power and press a small country into granting concessions?

Why is it that we do not see dominant powers, like Britain in the nineteenth century and ourselves after World War II, pursue a selfish economic policy but instead pursue a liberal trade policy?

I think the answer is, as he said, that trade negotiations are much more than just exchanges of economic concessions. The

Cooper point is that trade policy is foreign policy. When you are a hegemonic power, as we were after World War II, we could give concessions to all countries and follow the MFN principle because our political, military, and economic interests other than trade were worldwide so that we were reaping benefits politically throughout the world. We could therefore give trade concessions that went all over the world.

Now as the United States has declined in power, it is not surprising to see that we are moving more towards a bilateral approach. Now we don't have power to exert military and political influence in certain parts of the world. But we do have power in North America and in certain areas in the Middle East. So we are willing to make trade concessions to these regions because there are foreign policy considerations driving relations with these regions.

We are going to see the Canadian agreement finally come down to foreign policy considerations.

So foreign policy and trade policy interests are tied closely. Sometimes we forget that, and, as I say, John made that point.

Now I want to talk about another issue, codes and also dispute resolution. The latter one I don't think we have talked about much today. I think that it is very much in the interests of the developing countries to pay attention to the code issues.

It is quite understandable why they don't because there is a public good problem there. The benefits of the codes go to everyone so it is not in the interest of any one single developing country to put a lot of resources into trying to figure out what is in its best interests.

The payoff to them is such that it doesn't warrant their paying attention to these collective issues. After all, most of them don't have the resources or diplomatic or economic specialists, to really become familiar with the issues and determine where their interests are. So this does suggest that some worthwhile activities can be done by A.I.D. or the World Bank, namely, to provide the institutional support for working on these collective good issues.

I gather there is a proposal by the World Bank trying to help the developing countries train their people for the Uruguay

Round negotiations, so that they know about such issues as dumping and subsidies.

I don't know how this proposal has fared. I know the World Bank is getting out a little book on the negotiations, but I doubt if it is going as far as it should. Hopefully, UNCTAD will also do something in this area.

This leads into the other issue, dispute resolution, which often comes up in connection with the codes. Many have been disappointed not only in the codes themselves but trying to get disputes resolved. However, we find what seems to be an imaginative new dispute settlement approach in the Canadian–U.S. free-trade agreement where there seems to be some sort of binding or semi-binding arbitration mechanism. I would like to hear more about it.

If we can do that with the United States and Canada, maybe we can use it to tighten the GATT. Everyone wants to strengthen the GATT, give more enforcement powers to it. Could that be a model for strengthening the GATT?

DR. MARES: I have a comment about what might be an impetus to developed country negotiations with developing countries and that is that this really might be a window of opportunity for securing liberalization in developing countries.

I get a sense in reading the three papers that there is a mistake, or at least from my perspective I see it as a mistaken belief, that somehow developing countries have learned that all of those protectionist policies were wrong.

In fact, if you look at Latin America since the late 1960s, we have been saying protectionist policies are bad, they lead to bottlenecks, et cetera, there are all these problems.

I think what we have to understand is that right now a lot of the liberalization, probably most of the liberalization, we see occurring in developing countries is as a result of the economic crisis that they happen to be in.

Since they liberalized, this could be a good time to bind them to that liberalization. That should be an impetus for developed country negotiators to see this as a unique opportunity to get developing countries to promise to continue with that liberalization.

Otherwise, we might go back into the cycle of liberalization, the crisis is over, then you get protection, another crisis, liberalization, et cetera.

MR. MASTERSON: Responding to your earlier question about how we can build more coalitions and get on from here, it seems to me that the economic interests of countries generally prevail. An exception can occur where concessions are made by one country to assist another and in so doing, foster more harmonious relations.

But having said that, the developing countries, I think, do have an economic self-interest to expand trade. While many of them may view themselves as importers or self-sufficient suppliers, most are already in an export position for one or more commodities or products. The export earnings are real to them. To accelerate the pace of economic growth, they must have access to the United States, to Japan, to Korea, to the Common Market, and to the other industrialized nations.

I think without a successful MTN, developing countries might find a trend towards bilateralism. The bilateralism would be between major exporters and importers and effectively exclude developing countries. We hope they see that it is in their economic interest to break out of what has been the normal pattern of going to GATT meetings and staying within a block of nonaligned parties. We encourage developing countries to join us in achieving a successful conclusion to the Uruguay Round.

Otherwise, I think we break into economic feudalistic states maintaining trade barriers with expensive, elaborate subsidy mechanisms. Even now we almost have new subsidy programs coming on stream faster than conferences can be called to study them. We have certainly done that in the last few years in the United States and Europe and the practice is spreading.

So those things, I would say, are very important. I do not know what the other alternatives would be in the event of a failure of this trade Round. Some would naturally advocate a market-sharing,

supply-management approach for agriculture. Or, in the industrialized area, we could fall into a more protectionistic environment
along the lines of last year's trade bill.

DR. WHALLEY: This is just a quick comment in response to
Anne's question about what kinds of initiatives would it make sense
for A.I.D. to consider. I am a foreigner so I shouldn't be offering
too much, but it does seem to me one major problem we are all
aware of in so many of these countries is a limited capacity to
negotiate. It is just so clear and stark in Africa, and then people
start talking in terms of resources and so on.

It seems to me that is a natural direction for A.I.D. to move in.
Perhaps I could just be a bit more specific. One recent initiative I
heard of which interested me greatly is that the ACP secretariat in
Brussels wants to follow the Uruguay Round collectively on behalf
of the ACP countries. Many of them are so small that they just
can't monitor it, they just can't follow it. It is really hopeless for
them to deal with it.

There is a lot of enthusiasm for that. I think there are 50 or 60
ACP countries but the secretariat will maintain a presence in Geneva.
It could be just information flows, their latest proposal, and so on
shipped out to the country, or it could even get more concrete.

It does seem to me that that is sensible given the size of these
countries and their ability to follow things. From a U.S. point of
view, presumably something like that for the CBI countries would
make a lot of sense because again, they are very small.

It is a bit different than the original Bank proposal which as I
understand it was to provide back-up support in Geneva with data
and people to whom countries could turn for advice. There the
assumption was that all the countries would walk into the Geneva
office and ask for this. This is a little bit different.

Then second, on a resource level, it seems to me, and this is a
comment perhaps more on Africa but it applies elsewhere, in many
of these countries people know very little about the multilateral
institutions. There is very little discussion of what their objectives
are, how the system works and so on.

I think you are looking at some kind of, I don't know what you would call it, training program or seminar series or whatever, but it has to go right down to the grass-roots level. You are talking about building up capability from a very, very, very low level. I am sure many of you would have imaginative plans as to how you would do that, but I think that has to be done in the countries rather than in Geneva.

Then finally, just in terms of resources for some of the poorer countries, you will hear them say, "Well, we don't go to meetings because we couldn't afford the plane fare. We get to Geneva and there is a meeting out of town and it is not just that we don't have a car, but the cab fare or the gas bills or whatever were too much." That suggests, of course, the need to target particular aid to some degree to just finance elevated participation in the Round. We will make available so many dollars for some trips and meetings and participation.

DR. PREEG: First, I want to say that I really appreciate the fact that we at A.I.D. are getting a lot of ideas and concepts thrown at us. I hope we are taking careful notes so that we can follow up. But I should also say that these are not all new ideas. We have been working in a lot of these areas, be it technical assistance where we can hire consultants, or some of the specific things we have been talking with the World Bank, the GATT, and others about.

We have been focusing to some extent on areas where our development assistance can help the process of adjustment to a more liberal trade regime. For example, in the Philippines, a country with which I happen to have been involved personally, the World Bank, in terms of trade liberalization, has a broad sectoral adjustment program to rationalize the import regime. It is also working on the sugar and coconut oil sectors, both major export commodities.

A.I.D., on the other hand, is supporting liberalization of fertilizer imports, phaseout of a parastatal monopoly for wheat imports, and freeing up of rice prices. We also support trade liberalization indirectly through strengthening rural infrastructure. Ed Schuh, I believe, made an important point this morning, that if you really want to open up and liberalize the agricultural sector, you need adequate infrastructure and financial intermediaries. Often it is the financing, and not just the money but the institutions, that is lacking. In the Philippines, the banks are in Manila, and you cannot create jobs in the provinces, nonagricultural as well as agricultural employment, without a strengthened financial structure.

There are a lot of development activities in the trade policy field. I am not convinced they are focused enough. Often we help trade liberalization without understanding the broader policy context. But there is a growing focus and a number of comments made here today are very well taken.

Now if I might respond to two of the broad questions that Anne threw out. One relating to the GATT Round is when do we get to the packaging stage. If anything, this Round is even more dispersed than previous ones, with 16 negotiating groups and other issues that fall between the cracks and have not yet been addressed.

My own feeling is that it is too early for attempting a package. One has to see which issues will develop further in coming months. The services negotiating group has made progress that may surprise people that haven't been following it too closely. There is more common interest than anticipated, but concrete agreements are going to come later. Some issues where we need results need to be joined with those where others need something, and this will likely develop a little later. There still is the intent, however, to have some kind of midterm achievement, or early harvest, at the end of this year.

The second point is more fundamental, the question of systemic challenge to the trading system and the leadership role of the United States. A number of comments have been made about this. My personal assessment is that there are constraints to our leadership today that we didn't have 10, 20, or 30 years ago, in terms of bargaining leverage and our overall strength as a trading nation. Certainly our trade deficit is a constraint in terms of the way Congress and others look at what we are able to do internationally. On the A.I.D. side, too, in a number of areas, resources are a constraint to accomplishing our objectives.

Indeed, we have a certain amount of "chutzpah," at times, in the way we throw our policy weight around without resources. The Enhanced Structural Adjustment Fund, for example, which adds some six billion dollars of IME highly concessional lending for the poorest countries, is a case in point. We decided that we were not able to participate in the financing but we certainly have been involved in the whole process of creating ESAF.

In any event, I believe there is no real question that we want a strengthened GATT system. We have put a lot of weight and commitment behind the GATT Round and we are pushing ahead on all fronts. There is still considerable skepticism as to whether a major deal is feasible. There is skepticism about the European Community, and about Brazil, India, and some other LDCs. The developing countries seem to be requesting unilateral concessions, based on S&D, with little indication of their participation.

In parallel, bilateral trade relations are moving ahead with Canada and Mexico, and in a very tough but generally constructive way with Korea and Taiwan. The latter trading partners should be liberalizing in any event, and I will only make reference to a recent article by Secretary of the Treasury Baker.

It is in the magazine, *The International Economy,* and it is worth reading. It gives a positive perspective in seeing these bilateral negotiations as building blocks toward a multilateral liberal trading system. The result, however, could be a mix of bilateral, perhaps regional and multilateral relationships in which the multilateral dimension is the lowest common denominator.

In conclusion there is a highly complex set of relationships in terms of what we are after, and it is in that context that we need to address the systemic and leadership issues.

DR. MORSS: On the question of leadership, I would certainly caution A.I.D. people not go get out ahead of the administration on this liberalization issue. I think then you really have to ask yourself, what do you mean by the administration?

As I understand it, there is one view in the Commerce Department, and there is another view held by the undersecretary of the treasury, and the State Department (if it was ever asked) would have its own view, probably the most liberal of all.

My own interpretation of what happened is that the United States was under pressure to reduce its balance-of-payments deficit. It said we will do that but we recognize the global aggregate demand impact of doing so; it is up to us to coordinate our policies with the other Western nations.

The other Western nations really didn't come through, but the U.S. was still under pressure to reduce its balance-of-payments deficit, and it is now moving ahead with that to a greater or lesser degree in a manner that is not consistent with free-trade policies.

I think it is very dangerous and troubling and embarrassing if there is someone in A.I.D. who is doing something where the economic attache from the Embassy is down the street using absurd reasons for reducing the U.S. balance-of-payments position vis-à-vis that country. So I just think that there is a great danger in getting out in front of our policy on that.

DR. ORDEN: I want to come back to Mr. Venezia's engine room comment and see if I can tie a few things together by asking a question of the people from the engine room. The fact was spelled out in Professor Baldwin's paper that the United States has recently absorbed an enormous share of the growing exports from the developing countries. In spelling out this fact, nothing was stated about the size of recent U.S. trade deficits and what might happen to those proportions if the U.S. deficit were reduced and that is the issue that you raise.

If we can get back to a system of more or less balanced trade for the United States and other developed countries without a world recession which, in principle, is possible, then in principle also the developing countries should find other markets for some of the goods that they have been exporting to us.

In practice, if you think about this situation, as you obviously are, and think about where developing countries that you are dealing with are going to be when the trade balance comes around, as I think everyone recognizes it is going to at some point, then

A.I.D. might want to ask the countries with which it is working where do you find those other markets, or don't you. This might suggest some of the kinds of coalitions that you are talking about and some reasons for those coalitions that may not otherwise be apparent. We might get out of a North-South kind of discussion and into a discussion of the benefits of a liberalized trading world versus a restricted trading world. In such a discussion, we may find some partners that we would not otherwise have.

MR. VENEZIA: I would like only to clarify what I mentioned earlier when I used the word "client" and I am not sure that I was clear on that. The U.S. government is never a single entity. The U.S. government "are" and never "is." Many decisions on trade and investment that A.I.D. makes generally are made within the context of its impact on a U.S. supplier versus the recipient country.

Those pressures are clearly going to grow and shift, and when I say who is the client for A.I.D., I really mean not so much two individuals sitting in Thailand, I very much mean a supplier in Cleveland versus someone in Thailand.

It is clear in my mind that A.I.D. will be drawn very strongly to serving domestic interests far more than it is now doing.

Response

DR. FINCH: One very important issue has been focused by the comments of John Whalley. It is quite true that an important segment of developing country opinion differs from the approach we advocate. It fears open trading rules and favors opting out of the negotiation process. But we would stress that opinions are shifting in many of these countries toward interest in market access and that it is right to encourage further change. In particular, the trading environment in the coming years differs greatly from that of the last 40 years. There is much greater pressure for bilateral negotiation, and nontariff barriers largely operating without protective rules are now much more important. In our view developing countries need to recognize this weakness in the environment, and the consequent need for a strengthened GATT to give them assurance of fair treatment within agreed and enforced rules. As economists we stress the crucial importance of a receptive trading environment for these countries, as access to foreign markets is essential if they are ever to escape from poverty.

DR. MICHALOPOULOS: It is important for developing countries to negotiate actively in the Uruguay Round with the objective of improving their access to industrial countries' markets and strengthening the trading system in ways which are supportive of their interests. A stronger GATT Secretariat, a transparent safeguard system and an impartial and effective review mechanism are key improvements needed. Developing countries will not be able to achieve these objectives without commitments to reduce their own trade barriers and abide by GATT rules. These commitments should not be that onerous since a number of countries have found it advantageous to liberalize their trade not because of any obligations under the GATT, but because of their own development interest.

5

Anne O. Krueger

Conclusion:
A Policy Agenda

There is little question as to which issues in the international trading system are of major concern to the developing countries. They are, first and foremost, the restoration of a momentum toward trade liberalization and more rapid growth of the international economy. Within such a renewed momentum, removing barriers—principally NTBs—to the exports of developing countries' manufactured goods and agricultural products is clearly of great importance. There was an unusual degree of consensus among conference participants as to the types of agreements that would be most conducive to a desirable international trading system.

Much of the discussion in the final session focused on possible arrangements and mechanisms that might achieve the desired outcome, as well as the obstacles that stand in the way of success. This final chapter provides an overview of that discussion and the issues that were raised. A first section briefly reiterates the main points of agreement as to desirable objectives that emerged from the Baldwin, Johnson, and Finch and Michalopoulos papers and comments on them. Thereafter, there is an analysis of some of the possible negotiating mechanisms that might assist in achieving those objectives, as well as of some of the obstacles perceived to be diminishing the likelihood of a rapid restoration of momentum toward an open, multilateral trading system.

Opportunity for Mutual Gain

There was virtual unanimity among participants in support of Johnson's view that restraining domestic policies that sustain inefficient agriculture in the developed countries is desirable from the viewpoint of the industrial countries themselves. It would also serve the interests of the developing countries. Although there would be need for an adjustment period during which a transition to more open policies could be effected, there would be significant increases in economic efficiency within the industrial countries. Since price support programs benefit large farms and large-scale farming more than small farmers, efficiency gains would not be at the expense of income distribution.

Such a liberalization of domestic agricultural policies would be much easier for the industrial countries to undertake if all adopted these policies at the same time. Moreover, participants accepted Johnson's warning that the current danger is that the present inefficient system of subsidizing agricultural producer prices could be "built in" to the system and become even more difficult to ameliorate if "supply management" practices, which now appear to be increasing in favor, become entrenched.

The net result of liberalization would be significant benefits for exporters of temperate agricultural crops (see Johnson's estimates regarding the order of magnitude of possible price changes), since the prices of those crops could be expected to increase on world markets as the industrial countries ceased their practice of subsidized exporting.[1]

Likewise, liberalizing trade in manufactures, and especially removing nontariff barriers in clothing and textiles and other labor-intensive commodities, would result in sizable gains for developing countries whose comparative advantage within manufacturing clearly lies largely in production of relatively labor-intensive commodities. In the short run, the established exporters of textiles and clothing, such as Korea and Hong Kong, might lose under a liberalization of trade in those commodities, as they would lose quota-rents. But, their gains from the more open international economy would surely provide an offset. It also can be argued that their own economic growth will depend crucially on their ability and willingness to accept the gradual shrinkage of their older industries.

In the present environment, agreements protecting would-be entrants into new markets from the threat of bilateral protectionist measures would themselves be beneficial to developing countries, as well as to developed countries. Indeed, as Baldwin argued, perhaps the greatest incentive for the developing countries to attempt to stimulate action and agreement in the present Round of trade negotiations is that the alternative will almost certainly be bilateral bargaining.

Need for Developing Countries' Participation

The urgent necessity of regaining lost momentum in liberalizing the international economy is not, at least to date, matched by concrete proposals as to how this might be achieved, even for trade among the developed countries. Despite the progress represented by formation of the Cairns Group, and by the recognition of the importance of the developing countries implicit in the name of the new Round of trade negotiations, there remain a great many obstacles to achieving agreement on liberalization, especially for items of interest to developing countries.

The fact is that the developing countries have become sufficiently important as trading partners that their participation will make a significant difference to the likelihood of a successful conclusion of the Uruguay Round. To be sure, except that there is a common (and overriding) interest in the overall growth of international trade, different groups of developing countries have different interests. The NICs' main concern is to maintain access and reduce barriers to their exports of manufactured products to the industrial countries' markets. The lower income developing countries have a substantial interest in the liberalization of trade in labor-intensive commodities. And the predominantly agricultural exporters among the developing countries have an interest in the liberalization of that trade, not only in temperate commodities, but also in sugar, edible oils, and numerous processed agricultural products.

The urgency and magnitude of the gains that could result, were these interests realized, is so great that it raises serious questions as to whether developing countries are well advised to continue to press for special and differential treatment in the GATT. Indeed, given that their own economic growth will probably be conditioned by the degree to which they liberalize their trade regimes, it is apparent that a major issue is how that liberalization—which is taking place bilaterally and without "trading concessions"—can be used to achieve the desired reductions in the industrial countries' trade barriers toward imports from developing countries.

Domestic Obstacles to Achieving Multilateral Trade Liberalization

This set of questions naturally turns attention to the obstacles to achieving mutually beneficial trades. Since the Uruguay Round is underway, and is the mechanism that it is hoped will achieve the desired resumption of momentum toward an open, multilateral trading system, the discussion focused on the problem of identifying mechanisms that currently obstruct resolution of the key issues and simultaneously suggesting techniques for achieving a better outcome.

There are two distinct sets of issues: those affecting individual countries' internal policy processes, and those affecting international decisions on trade issues. Much of the discussion in the concluding session focused on these issues.

Within countries, there are a number of considerations, both political and institutional, that probably bias the policymaking process toward greater protection than would otherwise result. There is, first of all, the tendency of politicians and voters alike to "see" the economic interests they are protecting but to fail to see the interests they are deprotecting. While it is a widely accepted economic truth that protection of some interests is deprotection of others, those supporting protectionism for a particular product usually fail to recognize that the effect will be, among other things, for the exchange rate to appreciate somewhat, with consequent pressure on export industries and import-competing industries not subject to protection. When exporters' profits are reduced, their expansion plans are delayed or abandoned, but the individuals who might have had jobs in the export activity do not themselves know who they are.

Secondly, there is probably a tendency within the political process to blame foreigners to a greater extent than is warranted. For example, it can easily be demonstrated that protection extended to American textile interests resulted in a more rapid shift of domestic production from North to South than would otherwise have occurred: the relatively greater profitability of production in the American South was clearly an important factor in the reduction of employment and the closing of plants in the North. Yet, despite that, New England interests supported protection of domestic textile production from foreign competition, underestimating the extent that their difficulties originated in domestic competition and failing to recognize that higher textile prices would induce more investment and a more rapid shift to the South than would have occurred without protection.

In other industries seeking protection and blaming foreign competition for employment losses and other dislocations, it often turns out to be slow productivity growth, or failure of demand growth that accounts for much of the problem. Yet, imports get blamed. While there is little question that imports contribute to the difficulty of industries under competitive pressure, they are seldom as important a source of difficulty as is popularly thought. Moreover, protectionist measures very often fail to correct the situation and can indeed exacerbate it.

Both of these biases can be mitigated to the extent that the public and politicians are well informed about the economic processes affecting their fortunes. Analyses of the costs of protection can support efforts of those attempting to thwart protectionist pressures.

Another source of bias, however, is institutional in nature, and it is much more difficult to suggest possible remedies. In almost all countries, trade policy with respect to manufactured commodities is the responsibility of one ministry, while trade policy vis-à-vis domestic agriculture is the responsibility of another. The result is that it is difficult to effect trade-offs between a country's manufacturer and farmer interests—decision making is at a level on which only trade-offs within agriculture and manufacturing can be considered. Especially for the industrial countries, where there are widely recognized potential gains to be had from liberalization of trade in manufactures, the institutional difficulties associated with this compartmentalization of trade policy are serious.

International Obstacles to Achieving a Multilateral Trade Bargain

It is the existence of domestic political pressures, and the biases in them, that led officials to use an international organization, and the "trading" of concessions, as a mechanism to resist protectionism. To the extent that a policymaker may resist pressures for protection "because we are bound under international law," or because he can show the benefits of the reciprocal trade concessions to those who otherwise would not "be seen," the mechanism of reciprocal negotiations for reductions of trade barriers provides an offset to the political biases inherent in domestic political structures.

Nonetheless, there are institutional difficulties internationally. First and foremost, all participants agreed that protectionist pressures in the United States and other industrial countries are intensified to the extent that there are marked fluctuations in real exchange rate relations among them. Clearly, protectionist pressures in the United States increased rapidly when the real value of the U.S. dollar appreciated sharply in the early 1980s. While it is to be hoped that the underlying monetary-fiscal policies of the industrial countries will be so conducted as to avoid a repetition of those sharp swings in real rates, it must be recognized that the international financial relationships strongly affect the degree of protectionist pressures within the industrial countres. From the viewpoint of the international economy, perhaps the single most important policy step that might be taken to foster growth of an open multilateral trading system would be to address and correct the causes of the current macroeconomic imbalances within the industrial countries—a task institutionally far removed from those responsible for implementation of trade policy.

Second, there is the historical stance of the developing countries supporting their S&D status. Considerable attention was devoted during the final conference session to this stance and the reasons for it. It was pointed out that the historical unanimity of developing countries in support of S&D status has crumbled as the NICs and other developing countries have recognized where their greater interest lies. Even so, a number of developing countries continue to believe that the benefits they receive, for example, under GSP, are greater than the gains they could achieve through multilateral trade negotiations and reductions of trade barriers across all countries.

Related to this is a second institutional issue: given that developing countries, like developed countries, do not have entirely coincident interests, how can multilateral tariff negotiations be structured in order to permit them to participate? Participants noted that the GATT had been a most effective forum for multilateral reductions when the primary issue was tariffs and when a small number of large trading nations were involved in the negotiations. Then, it was relatively straightforward for the United States, for example, to reach agreement with Japan over a particular set of tariff reductions, and then for the U.S. and Japan each to bargain with the

EC countries for their "compensating" tariff reduction. As the number of trading countries with substantial interests in the system has increased, it has become more difficult for small trading nations to negotiate; having over 90 countries in GATT each engaging in bilateral bargains is very unwieldy.

A number of participants also pointed to the apparent paradox of the large industrial countries simultaneously erecting protectionist trade barriers vis-à-vis developing countries and then being concerned that the heavily indebted among the developing countries increase their exports in order to grow and service their debts. If there were mechanisms to link the foci on trade issues with those on agricultural policies and those affecting finance, it was thought that the chances of finding a formula for achieving a significant reversal of protectionist pressures and liberalization of trade would be much greater.

Finally, international institutional issues were raised. On one hand, the IMF conducts surveillance of trade and exchange rate policies with individual member countries, while the GATT's own surveillance mechanisms are rather weak. On the other hand, the IMF and the World Bank often work with governments of developing countries for policy reforms that will improve their growth prospects. These reforms usually include substantial elements of trade liberalization. It was noted by one participant that some developing countries had even removed quantitative restrictions and had reduced their highest tariff rates to less than 25 percent without any reciprocity from their trading partners. As Finch and Michalopoulos noted, a mechanism to insure credit for these unilateral trade liberalizing reforms is highly desirable.

Scope for Global Gain

If means could be found, there is a remarkable opportunity for a global compact, which would significantly enhance the growth prospects of all nations. This compact would include assurances by the industrial countries that their markets would be open and, indeed, that existing nontariff barriers to trade would be removed for both agricultural and nonagricultural trade.[2] The NICs would benefit greatly from those assurances and could, in return, remove their remaining protectionist barriers against imports of labor-intensive goods, as well as continue to liberalize their trade regimes. Those developing countries that have established sizable manufacturing industries would benefit from increased market access, and could gradually reduce and then eliminate their trade barriers to imports of capital-intensive products. To the extent that those countries are unilaterally doing so out of self-interest, procedures could and should be established so that they could get credit for binding their tariffs to low levels.

Clearly, if NICs were to liberalize in step with developed countries, the pressure on the latters' markets in labor-intensive manufactures would be considerably less than it would be were the industrial countries only to liberalize. Likewise, coordinated reduction of price supports to agriculture among the developed countries would greatly reduce the required adjustment that would result from a unilateral removal of supports on the part of any one of them. And, were the poorer countries with sizable manufacturing sectors to liberalize their imports of manufactures, while simultaneously attaining increased market access for their products in the industrial countries and the NICs, the transition problems they would confront would be substantially less than they would be with unilateral liberalization.

Thus, the case for a coordinated move toward trade liberalization is compelling. To get there will clearly require several things: 1) the negotiation of a safeguards clause enforceable within the GATT that is deemed acceptable by the industrial countries; 2) development of a mechanism or mechanisms for the formation of groups, such as the Cairns Group, so that nations sharing a common interest may work jointly in pursuit of those interests; 3) creation of a formula, or formulae, for removal of quantitative restrictions to trade and domestic subsidies that affect international trade (such as in agriculture); 4) achievement of agreement on codes of conduct that will provide transparency for countries' protectionist measures; and 5) the political will, or vision, to carry this out.

The negotiation of a reasonable safeguards clause within the GATT, as discussed by Baldwin, was judged by most participants to be essential politically if there is to be any hope of a negotiated broad reduction of trade barriers. In the absence of such a measure, industrial countries are deemed likely to persist in taking protectionist measures outside the GATT framework.

The need for finding institutional means for permitting groups of countries to negotiate jointly over those items in their common interest (such as the Cairns Group) has already been stressed. While the sheer number of countries involved will dictate such an approach, it will be equally important that countries be willing to trade off some of their interests in one sector (services, agriculture, manufactures, etc.) against their interests in other traded items.

Finding formulae for reduction and elimination of nontariff barriers is clearly essential if a large number of countries are to negotiate liberalization of their trade regimes. The OECD has already proposed the "producer subsidy equivalent" measure for agricultural trade, although other approaches are possible. On the industrial side, there is historical precedent in the negotiated liberalization of Japanese trade, and also in the liberalization of intra-European trade that took place after the Second World War. Finding a means of quantification of existing trade barriers will be a necessary starting point if formulae for their reduction and elimination are to be found.

In this connection, many conference participants stressed the point that efforts to find formulae and mechanisms for multilateral reduction of trade barriers will inevitably demand considerable technical expertise. Trade barriers are by their nature complex, and assessing the implications of alternative formulae is a difficult technical task. Many participants pointed out that developing countries, and especially the small ones, could benefit greatly if A.I.D., or one of the international institutions, were to provide technical assistance to those developing countries that desired it.

Related to that issue was the great desirability of strengthening the GATT Secretariat. Not only would this permit increased surveillance by GATT staff of member countries' trade practices, possibly in itself providing greater discipline, but it would be essential were the GATT Secretariat to be in a position to oversee negotiated liberalization of NTBs.

As already stressed, all countries would then be expected to participate in trade liberalization. It might, however, be negotiable as to the time-phasing and extent of liberalization expected of different parties. For example, once having agreed to a procedure for quantifying nontariff barriers to trade in manufactures, it might be agreed that industrial countries would eliminate their NTBs by reducing them $100/x$ percentage points per year over x years, while NICs might reduce them $100/y$ percentage points a year over y years and poorer developing countries might take even longer, and perhaps be left with some degree of permitted residual protection.[3]

The need for transparency was repeatedly stressed throughout the conference. Once government policies become opaque and cover the gamut of interventions, it becomes impossible for countries to agree upon rules of the game and use GATT dispute settlement resources for cases when differences arise. Only if countries agree to codes of conduct that essentially insure that they will not undertake measures whose protective content is difficult or impossible to detect or assess, will it be possible to negotiate and implement formulae of the type envisaged herein.

The fifth and final essential, the political will, in many ways seems the most elusive. In the wrap-up session, some participants decried the apparent abdication of the United States as a leader with a hegemonic interest in an open, liberal trading system. Others saw the failure of the United States to support the open, multilateral system as aggressively as had been the case in earlier years, as a consequence of the changed American economic status in the world. Regardless of the cause, the fact that there appears to be something of a leadership vacuum in the international economy is clearly a negative factor in influencing the likelihood of successfully resuming the momentum to trade liberalization.

For reasons indicated above, the participants were not overly sanguine that the current Round of trade negotiations would achieve the desired result. Some participants believed that it is too early in the Uruguay Round to witness any concrete proposals and that, as the Round proceeds and discussions progress, particular concrete proposals will be evaluated and possibly adopted. The major basis for optimism, it was agreed, was that the alternative to success of the new Round is so very bleak that nations will, when confronted directly with it, recognize their common interest in an open, multilateral trading system under recognized rules and procedures for dispute settlement through the GATT. For the developing countries, the failure of the Uruguay Round will probably lead to greater emphasis on bilateral negotiations over the trade and capital flows—a prospect that may be regarded as sufficiently unpleasant as to lead them to embrace the multilateral system with greater enthusiasm than has historically been the case. Whether developed and developing countries will recognize the disastrous alternative during the Uruguay Round, or whether it will be triggered by other events, is a question whose answer will be known only in the future.

Notes and References

1. Anne O. Krueger, Introduction

I am grateful to David Finch, D. Gale Johnson, and Constantine Michalopoulos for helpful comments on an earlier draft of this paper.

1. The reader interested in background on the GATT can consult Dam and Congressional Budget Office.

2. For an account of the origins of GATT, see Dam. The developing countries opposed the formation of the ITO for reasons similar to their later resistance to GATT.

3. There was also provision for temporary protection in instances in which a country, having reduced its protection, found its domestic economy seriously "injured" due to import penetration. These provisions, known as "safeguards," influence a variety of issues in international economic relations, but for present purposes they are important because there is a major dispute between developed and developing countries over whether the application of safeguards might be country-specific (as advocated by most developed countries) or nondiscriminatory in their application. See Baldwin's chapter in this volume for a fuller discussion.

4. A "bound" tariff is one which may not be increased (except under certain special circumstances to be noted below) because it was negotiated to the "bound" level under multilateral tariff negotiations or upon accession to GATT; in either circumstances, the country is prevented from raising the tariff by its obligations under GATT. A "bound" tariff may be increased

only if suitable "compensation" is offered through trade liberalization of some other commodity or commodities of interest to the countries exporting the item whose binding is lifted.

5. Note that economic analysis demonstrates that, in all but special circumstances, free trade (and hence tariff reduction) is in the self-interest of any country, and countries should thus be interested in unilateral tariff reductions. The GATT, however, provides a mechanism whereby tariff reductions are "traded" among countries—a process consistent with a more mercantilist view of the benefits of trade. It might be argued, however, that if political pressures for protection arise within individual countries, the mechanisms of the GATT and reciprocal tariff reduction provide an institution to assist in resisting those pressures within national governments.

6. See Baldwin 1970, p. vii.

7. See GATT 1979 for a description of the major codes negotiated during the Tokyo Round.

8. Some very prominent developing countries, including Mexico and China, did not accede to the GATT until the 1980s.

9. See Baldwin 1969 for an analysis of the circumstances under which the infant industry argument might be appropriate.

10. For a discussion of the Generalized System of Preferences and their effects on developing countries, see Wolf 1984.

11. See Wolf 1986.

12. Countries adopting import substitution also almost invariably neglected productivity increasing investments in agriculture in their focus on industrialization. Experience has demonstrated that growth cannot for long be sustained unless rural productivities increase pari passu with urban productivity. For a recent exposition of this view, see Schultz.

13. In many developing countries, initial levels of protection were greatly heightened when balance-of-payments difficulties arose; actual levels of protection were well in excess of those initially advocated on import substitution grounds. See, for example, Bhagwati and Srinivasan on India.

14. The interested reader can consult Bhagwati 1978 and Krueger 1978, 1983 for further analysis.

15. For a survey of the evidence with respect to export-promoting trade strategies, see Bhagwati 1988 and the references therein.

16. For further analysis of these issues, see World Bank 1987.

17. For a series of papers addressing the issues of the new Round in greater depth from the viewpoint of the developing countries, see Finger and Olechowski.

18. See World Bank 1986 for an analysis of developing countries' agriculture in a global context.

References

Baldwin, Robert E. 1969. The case against infant industry protection. *Journal of Political Economy* 77(3).

Baldwin, Robert E. 1970. *Nontariff Distortions of International Trade.* Washington, D.C.: Brookings Institution.

Bhagwati, Jagdish N. 1988. Export-promoting trade strategy: Issues and evidence. *The World Bank Research Observer* 3, no. 1.

Bhagwati, Jagdish N. 1978. *Foreign Trade Regimes and Economic Development: Anatomy and Consequences of Exchange Control.* Lexington, MA: Ballinger Press for the National Bureau of Economic Research.

Bhagwati, Jagdish, and T. N. Srinivasan. 1975. *Foreign Trade Regimes and Economic Development: India.* New York: Columbia University Press for the National Bureau of Economic Research.

Congress of the United States, Congressional Budget Office. 1987. *GATT Negotiations and U.S. Trade Policy.* Washington, D.C.: U.S. Government Printing Office.

Dam, Kenneth W. 1970. *The GATT Law and International Economic Organization.* Chicago: University of Chicago Press.

Finger, J. Michael, and Andrzej Olechowski, eds. 1987. *The Uruguay Round: A Handbook on the Multilateral Trade Negotiations.* Washington, D.C.: World Bank.

General Agreement on Tariffs and Trade. 1979. *Agreements Relating to the Framework for the Conduct of International Trade.* Geneva: GATT.

Krueger, Anne O. 1978. *Foreign Trade Regimes and Economic Development: Liberalization Attempts and Consequences.* Lexington, MA: Ballinger Press for the National Bureau of Economic Research.

Krueger, Anne O. 1983. *Trade and Employment in Developing Countries.* Chicago: University of Chicago Press for the National Bureau of Economic Research.

Schultz, T. W. 1988. The long view in economic policy: The case of agriculture and food. International Center for Economic Growth, Occasional Paper No. 1. San Francisco: Institute for Contemporary Studies Press.

World Bank. 1986. *World Development Report 1986.* Washington, D.C.: World Bank.

World Bank. 1987. *World Development Report 1987.* Washington, D.C.: World Bank.

Wolf, Martin. 1984. Two-edged sword: Demands of developing countries and the trading system. In Jagdish Bhagwati and John G. Ruggie, eds. *Power, Passions, and Purpose: Prospects for North-South Negotiations.* Cambridge: MIT Press.

Wolf, Martin. 1987. Diffential and more favorable treatment of developing countries and the international trading system. *World Bank Economic Review* 1, no. 4.

2.   **D. Gale Johnson, Policy Options and Liberalizing Trade in Agricultural Products: Addressing the Interests of Developing Countries**

1.   Section 22 was enacted in 1951 after the United States was found guilty by GATT of imposing quantitative import restrictions on dairy products in violation of Article XI of GATT. Section 22 required the executive to impose quantitative restrictions or special fees whenever "any article or articles are practically certain to be imported into the United States under such conditions and in such quantities as to render or tend to render ineffective or materially interfere with" any U.S. farm program. Interference has been interpreted broadly to include any significant increase in governmental expenditures required to carry out the purpose of farm programs.

2.   In 1955 the United States requested and obtained a waiver of its obligations under Article XI of GATT. While the title of this article is "General Elimination of Quantitative Restrictions," it was written to permit the use of quantitative restrictions for agricultural products, if certain conditions were met. One of the conditions was that domestic production was to be reduced and imports could not be reduced by more than domestic production. The United States imposed strict controls on dairy products—and still does—but made no pretense to limit the output of milk until 1984. There was no time limit imposed when the waiver was granted, and the United States does not have to justify its use of the waiver.

3.   In 1983, due to the rapid accumulation of stocks of wheat, feed grains, and cottons under the 1981 and 1982 farm price support program, an effort was made to achieve a large reduction in farm crop production. Nearly 65 million acres or nearly one-fifth of all cropland was idled. In an effort to speed the disposal of the large stocks owned by the federal government, a large fraction of the payments made to farmers was made in kind—in wheat, feed grains, or cotton. Thus the program was known as Payment-in-Kind, or PIK for short.

4.   As John Floyd showed over two decades ago in an article sadly neglected by both policymakers and economists, if the elasticity of supply of purchased inputs approaches infinity, and if such inputs account for a large share of total inputs, the long-run elasticity of supply of farm output will exceed unity even if the elasticity of substitution between farm- and nonfarm-supplied inputs is quite low and if the elasticity of supply of farm-supplied inputs (land, labor, and management) is as low as 0.1 or 0.2. Assuming an elasticity of substitution as low as 0.5, purchased inputs at 65 percent of total inputs and an elasticity of supply of farm-supplied inputs of 0.2, the long-run elasticity of supply of farm output would be 1.5, several times the 0.3 assumed by Andy

Stoeckel. (See page 33 of this volume.) Even if you reduce the elasticity of substitution to 0.2 and assume that the elasticity of supply of farm-supplied inputs is 0.1, the long-run elasticity of output supply is in excess of 0.5.

The formula for this result, which is implicit in the article by Floyd, is $e = (K_c\alpha_c + \beta_c)/(1 - K_c)$ as the elasticity of supply of farm output (c); α_c is the elasticity of substitution between purchased and farm-supplied inputs; β_c is the elasticity of supply of farm-supplied inputs; and K_c is the share of purchased inputs in total inputs.

5. The tax treatment of farm land in Japan discourages the transfer of land from agriculture to nonagricultural uses. Even when the farm land has a valuable nonfarm use, such as the rice paddies in the city of Tokyo, the land is taxed not in terms of its market value but on the basis of its value as farm land. In spite of some efforts to reduce the barriers imposed by the basic land reform law upon the purchase and sale of farm land and the renting of such land, there remain many impediments to farm enlargement that is required if Japanese agriculture is to become significantly more efficient.

6. Higher farm prices do increase the return to land and in this way will increase the incomes of some farm families, namely those families that owned land prior to the increase in farm prices. Families that rent land do not gain from the higher return to land nor do families that become land owners by purchasing land after a price support program has been inaugurated.

7. I am not arguing here or at the beginning of the paragraph that the trade negotiations should be based on achieving the same PSE level for all countries. My point is a simple one, namely that for at least many years to come, some positive level of average protection for all agricultural output will be required to permit a degree of protection for certain politically sensitive commodities. Unless such provision is made, there is little likelihood that any real progress can be made in the negotiations to reduce the barriers to trade in agricultural products.

References

Anderson, Kym, and Yujiro Hayami. 1986. *The Political Economy of Agricultural Protection*. London: Allen and Unwin.

Barney, G. O. 1982. *The Global 2000 Report to the President*. New York: Penguin Books.

Brechling, Jens, Sally Thorpe, and Andy Stoeckel. 1987. *Effects of EC Agricultural Policies: A General Equilibrium Approach. Initial Results*. Canberra: Bureau of Agricultural Economics.

Commission of the European Communities. 1981. *Guidelines for European Agriculture*. Brussels, COM(81) 608 final.

Dvoskin, Dan. 1988. *Excess Capacity in U.S. Agriculture: An Econometric Approach to Measurement.* Economic Research Service, U.S. Department of Agriculture, Agric. Econ. Rpt. No. 580.

Floyd, John E. 1965. The effects of farm price supports on the returns to land and labor in agriculture. *Journal of Political Economy* 73, no. 2: 148-58.

Hathaway, Dale. 1987. *Agriculture and GATT: Rewriting the Rules.* Washington, D.C.: Institute for International Economics.

Johnson, D. Gale. 1973. *Farm Commodity Programs: An Opportunity for Change.* Washington, D.C.: American Enterprise Institute.

_____. 1975. World agriculture, commodity policy, and price variability. *American Journal of Agricultural Economics* 57, no. 5: 34-40.

_____. 1982. International trade and agricultural labor markets: Farm policy as quasi-adjustment policy. *American Journal of Agricultural Economics* 61, no. 2: 353-461.

_____. 1984. Domestic agricultural policy in an international environment: Effects of other countries' policies on the United States. *American Journal of Agricultural Economics* 66, no. 5: 735-44.

_____. 1986. Food security and Japanese agricultural policy. *Issues in U.S.-Japan Agricultural Trade.* New York: Carnegie Council on Ethics and International Affairs.

Johnson, D. Gale, Kenzo Hemmi, and Pierre Lardinois. 1985. *Agricultural Policy and Trade: Adjusting Domestic Programs in an International Framework.* New York: New York University Press.

Mayer, Leo V., Earl O. Heady, and Howard C. Madsen. 1968. *Farm Programs for the 1970s.* Center for Agricultural and Economic Development, Report No. 32, Iowa State University.

Miller, Geoff. 1986. *The Political Economy of International Agricultural Policy Reform.* Canberra: Australian Government Publishing Service.

Organisation for Economic Co-operation and Development (OECD). 1984. *Issues and Challenges for OECD Agriculture in the 1980s.* Paris: OECD.

_____. 1987. *National Policies and Agricultural Trade.* Paris: OECD.

Paarlberg, Robert L. 1986. *Fixing Farm Trade: Policy Options for the United States.* New York: Council on Foreign Relations.

Quance, Leroy, and Luther Tweeten. 1972. Excess capacity and adjustment potential in U.S. agriculture. *Agricultural Economics Research* 24, no. 36.

Tyers, Rod, and Kym Anderson. 1986. Global interactions and trade liberalization in agriculture. Revised April 1987. Background paper for World Bank, *World Development Report 1986.* New York: Oxford University Press.

Tyner, F. H., and L. G. Tweeten. 1964. Excess capacity in U.S. agriculture. *Agricultural Economics Research* 16, no. 1.

U.S. Department of Agriculture. 1987. *World Agriculture: Situation and Outlook Report.* WAS-49 and WAS-50.

_____. 1986. *Agricultural Outlook*. A0-123.

_____. 1987. *Feed: Situation and Outlook*. Fds-304.

Valdes, Alberto. 1987. Agriculture in the Uruguay Round: Interests of developing countries. *The World Bank Economics Review* 1, no. 4: 570-94.

Valdes, Alberto, and Joachim Zietz. 1980. *Agricultural Protection in the OECD Countries: Its Cost to Less Developed Countries*. Washington, D.C.: International Food Policy Research Institute.

World Bank. 1986. *World Development Report 1986*. New York: Oxford University Press.

3. Robert E. Baldwin, Increasing Access to Markets for Manufactured Goods: Opportunities in the Uruguay Round

1. The share for 1963 is based on Appendix Table I.1 in Blackhurst, Marian, and Tumlir (1978). The 1984 figure is from Sampson (1986).
2. This figure and the date on U.S. import shares are from Sampson (1986).
3. For a well-reasoned set of arguments for changing GATT safeguard rules to permit selectivity, see Wolff (1983).

References

Blackhurst, Richard, Nicolas Marian, and Jan Tumlir. 1978. *Adjustment, Trade and Growth in Developed and Developing Countries*. Geneva: General Agreement on Tariffs and Trade.

Sampson, Gary. 1986. Structural change: Accommodating imports from developing countries. Paper presented at International Economics Study Group conference, "Causes of Changes in the Structure of International Trade," September 5-7, 1986, Isle of Thorns, Sussex, England.

Wolff, Alan Wm. 1983. The need for new rules to govern safeguard actions. William R. Cline, ed. *Trade Policy in the 1980s*. Washington, D.C.: Institute for International Economics.

4. David Finch and Constantine Michalopoulos, Development, Trade, and International Organization

The authors wish to thank Shailendra J. Anjaria for his comments on an earlier draft of this paper. They are solely responsible for the views expressed in the paper which should not be interpreted to reflect the views of the World Bank.

1. These studies include Bela Balassa, "Structural Adjustment Policies in Developing Countries," *World Development* 10, no. 1 (1982):23-38; Michael Michaely, "Exports and Growth: An Empirical Investigation," *Journal of Development Economics* 4, no. 1 (March 1977):49-66; and Constantine Michalopoulos and Keith Jay, "Growth of Exports and Income in the Developing World: A Neoclassical View," *A.I.D. Discussion Paper No.*

28 (Washington, D.C.: Agency for International Development, 1973). See also, Paul Mosley, John Hudson, and Sarah Hozzell, "Aid, the Public Sector and the Market in Less Developed Countries," *Economic Journal* 97 (September 1987):616-641.

2.   A. O. Krueger and C. Michalopoulos, "Developing Country Trade Policies and the International Economic System," in E. Preeg, ed., *Hard Bargaining Ahead: US Trade Policy and Developing Countries* (Transaction Books for the ODC, 1985).

3.   The difficulties of designing tax cum subsidy policies to take advantage of external economies or market imperfections are outlined in Paul Krugman, "Is Free Trade Passé?" *Economic Perspectives* 1, no. 2 (Fall 1987):131-43. He concludes this review of modern attacks on the theory of comparative advantage by stating that "it is possible to believe that comparative advantage is an incomplete model of trade and to believe that free trade is nevertheless the right policy" (p. 143).

4.   World Bank, *World Development Report 1987.*

5.   Bela Balassa, "Exports, Policy Choices and Economic Growth in Developing Countries After the 1973 Oil Shock," *Journal of Development Studies* 18, no. 1 (June 1985):23-36.

6.   *World Development Report 1987.*

7.   Demetris Papageorgiou, Michael Michaely, and Armeane Choksi, "The Phasing of a Trade Liberalization Policy: Preliminary Evidence," World Bank, 1986 (mimeo).

8.   GATT Article XXVIII

9.   On this issue, see Martin Wolf, "Differential and More Favorable Treatment of Developing Countries and the International Trading System," *World Bank Economic Review* 1, no. 4 (September 1987).

10.   See C. Michalopoulos, "World Bank Programs for Adjustment and Growth," in V. Corbo, M. Goldstein, and M. Khan, *Growth Oriented Adjustment Programs* (IMF and World Bank, 1987).

11.   See in this volume Robert E. Baldwin, "Increasing Access to Markets for Manufacturing Goods: Opportunities in the Uruguay Round."

12.   There is a growing literature on the attitudes of developing countries on the issue of services. For a summary, see Jagdish N. Bhagwati, "Trade in Services and the Multilateral Trade Negotiations," *World Bank Economic Review* 1, no. 4 (September 1987).

13.   For a discussion of the advantages of reciprocal trade negotiations for such countries, see Bela Balassa and C. Michalopoulos, "Liberalizing Trade Between Developed and Developing Countries," *Journal of World Trade Law* 20, no. 1 (January 1986).

14.   On this issue, see C. Fred Bergsten, "Reforming the GATT: The Use of Trade Measures for Balance of Payments Purposes," *Journal of International Economics* 7(1977):1-18; also I. Frank, "Import Quotas, the Balance of Payments and the GATT," *World Economy* 10, no. 3 (September 1986); and S. Anjaria, "Balance of Payments and Related Issues in the Uruguay

Round of Trade Negotiations," *World Bank Economic Review* 1, no. 4 (September 1987).

5.   Anne O. Krueger, Conclusion: A Policy Agenda

1.   Some observers have questioned whether all developing countries would gain from agricultural trade liberalization. Some developing countries are grain importers and, they argue, grain importers would be likely to lose. Recently, however, Alberto Valdes has questioned this, noting that most studies of trade liberalization neglect tropical agriculture. See Alberto Valdes, "Agriculture in the Uruguay Round: Interests of Developing Countries," *World Bank Economic Review* 1, no. 4 (September 1987): 583. Moreover, even if there are developing countries that might lose on the higher prices for their agricultural imports, those countries would gain to some degree because of the benefits of more rapid overall growth of world trade that would result from liberalization.

2.   Even if NTBs were replaced with tariffs, that would be a useful starting point.

3.   There are numerous historical precedents for quantification. The major European countries agreed on a formula for estimating nontariff barriers after World War II, and proceeded to liberalize on that basis. The Japanese, likewise, liberalized a percentage of their nontariff barriers on a prenegotiated formula. More recently, the OECD proposed a "producer subsidy equivalent" as one possible formula for trade in agricultural commodities.

Contributors

Robert E. Baldwin is Hilldale Professor of Economics at the University of Wisconsin, Madison. He previously taught at Harvard and the University of California, Los Angeles. He was Chief Economist in the Office of the U.S. Trade Representative and a consultant to the United Nations Conference on Trade and Development, the World Bank, and the OECD. He is presently Director of the project on U.S. Trade Relations for the National Bureau of Economic Research. He is the author of *The Political Economy of U.S. Import Policy* (1985).

C. David Finch is a Senior Fellow at the Institute for International Economics. Before joining the Institute, he was on the staff of the International Monetary Fund from 1950 to 1987 where his most recent position was Counsellor and Director of the Exchange and Trade Relations Department. He has also served on the econometrics and statistics faculty at the University of Tasmania. His doctorate is from the London School of Economics.

D. Gale Johnson is the Eliakim Hastings Moore Distinguished Service Professor of Economics at the University of Chicago. Among his numerous affiliations outside the University, he has been a consultant to the Office of the President's Special Representative for Trade Negotiations, the Agency for International Development, and the U.S. Council on International Economic Policy; a member of the National Advisory Commission on Food and Fiber; and co-chairman of the Working Group on Population Growth and Economic Development for the National Research Council.

Anne O. Krueger is Arts and Sciences Professor of Economics at Duke University. Her former responsibilities include serving as Vice President, Economics and Research, at the World Bank and Professor of Economics at the University of Minnesota. She is a Research Associate of the National Bureau of Economic Research and was Director of the Bureau projects on Alternative Trade Strategies and Employment, and U.S. Trade Relations. She is co-editor, with Robert Baldwin, of *The Structure and Evolution of Recent U.S. Trade Policy* (1985).

Patrick Low is an economist with the General Agreement on Tariffs and Trade. He has been extensively involved with the negotiations at the Uruguay Round and during follow-up discussions.

Constantine Michalopoulos works at the World Bank as Economic Advisor to the Vice President for the European, Middle Eastern, and North African region. He formerly served as Chief Economist for the Agency for International Development, as Director of the International Development and Cooperation Agency, and as Associate Professor of Economics at Clark University in Massachusetts. His publications have concentrated on trade and financial policy issues related to development.

G. Edward Schuh is Dean of the Hubert H. Humphrey Institute of Public Affairs, University of Minnesota. Prior to assuming that position he was Director of Agriculture and Rural Development at the World Bank. He was a professor of Agricultural Economics at Purdue University, Program Advisor to the Ford Foundation in Brazil, Senior Staff Economist on the president's Council of Economic Advisors, Deputy Undersecretary for International Affairs and Commodity Programs at the U.S. Department of Agriculture, and Director of the National Bureau of Economic Research.

John Whalley is William G. Davis Professor of International Trade and Director of the Centre for the Study of International Economic Relations at the University of Western Ontario. He is also a Research Associate at the National Bureau of Economic Research. He has numerous publications in the areas of international trade, public finance, and general equilibrium analysis including *Dealing With the North: Developing Countries and the Global Trading System* (1987).

Participants

Duane Acker, A.I.D.
Garret Argento, A.I.D.
Robert Baldwin, University of Wisconsin
Alan Batchelder, A.I.D.
Charles Buchanan, A.I.D.
Malcolm Butler, A.I.D.
Stuart Callison, A.I.D.
David Carr, A.I.D.
John Chang, A.I.D.
Phillip Church, A.I.D.
John A. C. Conybeare, University of Iowa
Connie Corrino, A.I.D.
Michael Crosswell, A.I.D.
Ralph Cummings, A.I.D.
David Finch, Institute for International Economics
James Fox, A.I.D.
Mark Gallagher, A.I.D.
Mark Gellerson, A.I.D.
John Hardy, A.I.D.
Jerry Jenkins, Sequoia Institute
Frances Johnson, A.I.D.
D. Gale Johnson, University of Chicago
Kenneth Kauffman, A.I.D.
Anne O. Krueger, Duke University
Patrick Low, GATT (on leave)
David Mares, University of California at San Diego
Michael Masterson, A.I.D.
Donald McClelland, A.I.D.
Constantine Michalopoulos, World Bank
Elliott Morss, Boston University
James Mudge, A.I.D.
Bud Munson, A.I.D.
Eric Nelson, A.I.D.
P. J. Nichols, Department of State
David Orden, Virginia Polytechnic University
Ernest H. Preeg, A.I.D.
Sean Randolph
Miguel Rodriguez, Institute for International
    Economics

Dani Rodrik, Harvard University
Denise Rollins, A.I.D.
Edward Schuh, Hubert H. Humphrey Institute
Marilyn Seiver
Laura Sluka, The Heritage Foundation
Helen Soos, A.I.D.
Steven Sposato, A.I.D.
May Sue Talley, A.I.D.
Mike Unger, A.I.D.
Jan van der Veen, A.I.D.
Ron Venezia, A.I.D.
Carol Weber
Warren Weinstein, A.I.D.
John Whalley, University of Western Ontario
Ed Wise, A.I.D.
Neal Zank, A.I.D.

This book is a product of one of the seminars in a series addressing critical issues of foreign development and its assistance. The series, entitled,

INCLUDING THE EXCLUDED:
Extending the Benefits of Development

is conducted by Sequoia Institute, with the sponsorship of the Agency for International Development. The following individuals are members of the series' Academic Advisory Board: